MEASURING AND MANAGING

PERFORMANCE IN

ORGANIZATIONS

MEASURING AND MANAGING
PERFORMANCE IN
ORGANIZATIONS

ROBERT D. AUSTIN

foreword by Tom DeMarco & Timothy Lister

Dorset House Publishing
353 West 12th Street
New York, New York 10014

Library of Congress Cataloging-in-Publication Data

Austin, Robert D. (Robert Daniel), 1962-
    Measuring and managing performance in organizations / Robert D.
Austin ; foreword by Tom DeMarco & Timothy Lister.
        p.   cm.
    Includes bibliographical references and index.
    ISBN 0-932633-36-6
    1. Employees--Rating of.   I. Title.
HF5549.5.R3A927   1996
658.3' 125--dc20   96-9146
                                                                            CIP

Cover Design: Jeff Faville, FAVILLE DESIGN
Cover Photograph: JACK HARRISON PHOTOGRAPHY, Billericay, Essex, UK

Copyright © 1996 by Robert D. Austin. Published by Dorset House
Publishing Co., Inc., 353 West 12th Street, New York, NY 10014.

Distributed in the United Kingdom, Ireland, Europe, and Africa by
John Wiley & Sons Ltd., Chichester, Sussex, England. Distributed
in the English language in Singapore, the Philippines, and south-
east Asia by Toppan Co., Ltd., Singapore; and in the English language in Japan by Toppan Co., Ltd., Tokyo, Japan.

Printed in the United States of America

Library of Congress Catalog Number: 96-9146

ISBN: 0-932633-36-6   12 11 10 9 8 7 6 5 4 3 2 1

To Christopher and Warren

Acknowledgments

A great many people helped me, in one way or another, as I put this book together. Wendy Eakin, David McClintock, Ben Morrison, and the capable staff at Dorset House did much to improve the writing and the organization of this book. Pat Larkey, Robyn Dawes, Jay Kadane, and Steven Klepper, all Carnegie Mellon University professors and together an amazing mass of largely contrarian brain power, had much influence on the ideas in this book. Other CMU faculty who provided help, directly or indirectly, include Kristina Bichieri, Kathleen Carley, Paul Fischbeck, Mark Kamlet, John Miller, Teddy Seidenfeld, and Shelby Stewman. Thanks as well to Shmuel Zamir of Hebrew University at Jerusalem. Among my industrial colleagues, John Hrubes is notable for the quality of his ideas, many of which have found their way into this book. Ashish Sanil and Joe Besselman were valuable discussion partners who contributed their thoughts as well. To each of these people I owe very considerable thanks.

I also owe something to a pair of educational institutions. Carnegie Mellon University is a hot bed of original thought, where the best of the old and the new interact interestingly and fiercely, and where boundaries between fields are routinely and irreverently demolished. Swarthmore College, my original alma mater, provides perhaps the best and most strenuous undergraduate education in the known universe, and is like the most fun you can have while drinking directly from a firehose. I am enormously grateful that these two places exist and for the influence they had on me.

Thanks also to the eight software measurement experts who agreed to be interviewed for this book: David Card, Tom DeMarco, Capers Jones, John Musa, Dan Paulish, Larry Putnam, Ed Tilford, and an expert who decided to remain anonymous. Many people reviewed the manuscript at one time or another. Thanks to Martha Amis, Bill Barton, Rusty Lamont, Michael Mroczyk, and Kirk Zumhoff, all of whom spent time with early versions and provided support. Thanks to Bill Curtis who was extremely helpful until distance made our interactions less frequent.

And finally, to my family, I extend thanks. To my wife, Laurel, my daughter, Lillian, my brother, my parents—and to the many others who have helped me along in one way or another, or who regularly do so.

Permissions
Acknowledgments

The author and publisher gratefully acknowledge the following for their permission to reprint material quoted on the cited pages.

p. 3: Material reprinted by permission of *Harvard Business Review* from W. Bruce Chew, "No-Nonsense Guide to Measuring Productivity" (January-February 1988), p. 110; from Robert G. Eccles, "The Performance Manifesto" (January-February 1991), p. 131; and from Robert S. Kaplan and David P. Norton, "The Balanced Scorecard—Measures That Drive Performance" (January-February 1992), p. 71. Material reprinted by permission of *The Economist* from "The Death of Corporate Loyalty" (April 3, 1993), p. 63. Copyright © 1993 The Economist Newspaper Group, Inc. Reprinted with permission. Further reproduction prohibited.

p. 6: Material reprinted from "Dysfunctional Consequences of Performance Measurements" by V.F. Ridgway published in *Administrative Science Quarterly*, Vol. 1, No. 2 (September 1956), p. 243, by permission of Administrative Science Quarterly. Copyright © 1956 by Administrative Science Quarterly. Material reprinted by permission of *Harvard Business Review* from W. Bruce Chew, "No-Nonsense Guide to Measuring Productivity" (January-February 1988), p. 114.

p. 7: Material reprinted from "Dysfunctional Consequences of Performance Measurements" by V.F. Ridgway published in *Administrative Science Quarterly*, Vol. 1, No. 2 (September 1956), p. 247, by permission of Administrative Science Quarterly. Copyright © 1956 by Administrative Science Quarterly.

p. 10: Material reprinted by permission of The University of Chicago Press from Peter M. Blau, *The Dynamics of Bureaucracy: A Study of Interpersonal Relations in Two Government Agencies*, p. 10. Copyright © 1956, 1963. All rights reserved.

p. 11: Material reprinted by permission of The University of Chicago Press from Peter M. Blau, *The Dynamics of Bureaucracy: A Study of Interpersonal Relations in Two Government Agencies*, pp. 38, 50. Copyright © 1956, 1963. All rights reserved.

p. 17: Material reprinted by permission of The University of Chicago Press from Peter M. Blau, *The Dynamics of Bureaucracy: A Study of Interpersonal Relations in Two Government Agencies*, p. 52. Copyright © 1956, 1963. All rights reserved. Material from *Essays in the Theory of Risk-Bearing* (Markham, 1971) reprinted by permission of Kenneth J. Arrow.

p. 27: Material reprinted by permission of *Harvard Business Review* from Robert S. Kaplan and David P. Norton, "The Balanced Scorecard—Measures That Drive Performance" (January-February 1992), p. 72.

p. 28: Material reprinted by permission of Decision Sciences Institute at Georgia State University from Eric G. Flamholtz, "Toward a Psycho-Technical Systems Paradigm of Organizational Measurement," *Decision Sciences*, Vol. 10, No. 1 (January 1979), pp. 71–84.

p. 30: Material reprinted from "Dysfunctional Consequences of Performance Measurements" by V.F. Ridgway published in *Administrative Science Quarterly*, Vol. 1, No. 2 (September 1956), p. 247, by permission of Administrative Science Quarterly. Copyright © 1956 by Administrative Science Quarterly.

p. 71: Material reprinted by permission of *Harvard Business Review* from Robert G. Eccles, "The Performance Manifesto" (January-February 1991), p. 135.

pp. 85, 86: Material reprinted by permission of *The Economist* from "Diary of an Anarchist" (June 26, 1993), p. 66. Copyright © 1993 The Economist Newspaper Group, Inc. Reprinted with permission. Further reproduction prohibited.

pp. 86, 87: Material from "Chester I. Barnard and the Intelligence of Learning" by Barbara Leavitt and James G. March published in *Annual Review of Sociology*, Vol. 14 (1988), by permission of James G. March.

p. 130: Material from *Software Measurement Guidebook* copyright © 1992 Software Productivity Consortium Services Corp., Herndon, Va.

pp. 138–39: Material reprinted from "Notes on Ambiguity and Executive Compensation" by James G. March published in *Scandinavian Journal of Management Studies* (August 1984), pp. 57–58, by permission of James G. March.

pp. 142–44: Material from William G. Ouchi, *Theory Z: How American Business Can Meet the Japanese Challenge* (pp. 40-41, 48, and 58), ©1981 by Addison-Wesley Publishing Company, Inc. Reprinted by permission of the publisher.

p. 165: Material reprinted by permission of *The Economist* from "The Cracks in Quality" (April 18, 1992), p. 67. Copyright © 1992 The Economist Newspaper Group, Inc. Reprinted with permission. Further reproduction prohibited.

p. 179: Material from "The Firm Is Dead; Long Live the Firm, A Review of Oliver E. Williamson's *The Economic Institutions of Capitalism*" by Armen Alchian and Susan Woodward published in *Journal of Economic Literature*, Vol. 26 (March 1988), p. 77, by permission of Armen Alchian.

Contents

Foreword

One of the insights that comes early in a reading of Rob Austin's book, *Measuring and Managing Performance in Organizations,* is that measurement is a potentially dangerous business. When you measure any indicator of performance, you incur a risk of worsening that performance. This is what Rob calls *dysfunction.*

In order to see why this happens, you need to remember that measurement is almost always part of an effort to achieve some goal. You can't always measure all aspects of progress against the goal, so you settle for some surrogate parameter, one that seems to represent the goal closely and is simple enough to measure. So, for example, if the goal is long-term profitability, you may seek to achieve that goal by measuring and tracking productivity. What you're doing, in the abstract, is this:

measure **<parameter>** in the hopes of improving **<goal>**

When dysfunction occurs, the values of <parameter> go up comfortingly, but the values of <goal> get worse.

You probably understood long ago that dysfunction was a possibility, but thought—as we did—that it was nothing more than a rare, freakish anomaly. But as Rob pursues the subject with persuasive thoroughness, it gradually begins to dawn on you that dysfunction is not an exception to the rule; it is the rule: Anything you measure is likely to exhibit at least some dysfunction. When you try to measure performance, particularly the performance of knowledge workers, you're positively *courting* dysfunction.

Our first real understanding of dysfunction came from reading Rob's Ph.D. thesis. The thesis arrived at our offices over the transom (Tom had been interviewed for Rob's research project a year before, but did not even remember that when the thesis arrived), along with a pile of other hopeful contenders for our attention—brochures, monographs, phone and credit card bills, and a few book manuscripts. We dutifully looked through the first few pages, and then read the rest avidly. Recorded below, in abbreviated form, is the sequence of reactions that each of us had:

> *Why does this guy want me to read this thing? ...*
> *I see what he's getting at, but what does this have to do with me? ...*
> *Oh, I think I'm starting to see. ...*
> *Oh, oh. ...*
> *But surely this can't apply to the measurement that I'm doing. ...*
> *Gulp, it does. ...*

We called Rob for permission to make a few copies and sent them out, first to our fellow Guild members, and then to several influential members of the measurement community. As calls and email messages came back, we found that others were having the same response: "At first, I wondered why you wanted me to spend time on this huge pile of paper; by about page 30, I began to understand. ..."

When you realize that dysfunction will probably accompany almost any kind of measurement, you're inclined to ask questions like, Why and when is it likely to occur? What are the underlying causes? What are the indicators that it is happening? and, most of all, What can I do about it? Satisfying answers to these and other allied questions were provided by Rob's thesis, but by no other source that we knew of. That made us believe that the work needed to be made available in some more accessible form. We began to encourage and cajole Rob to develop his work into a book. *Measuring and Managing Performance in Organizations* is the admirable result. We believe this is a book that needs to be on the desk of just about anyone who manages anything.

June 1996

Tom DeMarco
Camden, Maine
Timothy Lister
New York, New York

Preface

Few management tools appear as simple and obviously useful as measurement. You establish numeric goals, take actions, and measure how the actions affect progress toward goals. Based on what the measures reveal, you adjust your actions. You continue in this way. Simple. You analyze measurements to determine what works and what doesn't. Despite organizational complexity, you learn confidently, your managerial decisions backed up by hard data. Obviously useful. Right?

Look more closely, however, and this clear picture begins to blur. Soon you find examples of measurement disaster. Look again and you discover startling disagreement among recognized experts about the value of organizational measurement. First, you encounter an expert who claims that measurement is indispensable, a nearly absolute good, almost a miracle cure. Next, you find an expert who concludes that measurement is inescapably harmful, a danger to the survival of the Western world, a seductive trap. Keep looking and you also see that, far from sorting out their differences, disagreeing experts seem to be largely ignoring each other. Your warm feelings of confidence in organizational measurement give way to cold misgivings.

This book is my attempt to sort it all out, to determine which organizational factors allow measurement to work successfully, and which force measurement programs to fail or do damage. Be forewarned, however: This is not a cookbook. You will not find quick-and-easy answers here. Measurement in organizations is not a quick-and-easy subject, and, as I will show, the idea that measurement is quick-and-easy causes quite a bit of trouble for people who try to implement measurement systems. What you will find in this book, I hope, is a way to deeper understanding of organizational measurement and a framework that will be useful as you consider measurement opportunities in your own organization. I hope that you find these things here, because the foremost goal of this book is to help managers and designers of real systems of measurement.

This book is different from some other books you might have read on measurement or related subjects. Perhaps the most important difference is in its emphasis on the behavioral aspects of measurement situations. There are no technical descriptions of specific measurements here and no details of measurement analysis or graphing techniques. Instead, the focus is on people and how they react when they are part of organizational systems that are being measured.

Another difference between this book and some others is its attention to measurement systems that don't work very well. Some books on measurement so strongly advocate its use that they look almost exclusively at success stories. They profess to tell you how to get it right, but they supply little or no detail about the consequences or likelihood of getting it wrong. Partly, this is because stories of management failures are harder to find than accounts of successes, for obvious reasons: People like to claim credit for successes and forget failures. But you can learn a lot from failure. So, I've worked to find examples of failure and devoted a significant portion of this book to examining the examples in search of a common pattern of failure. Understanding the pattern of failure can help us avoid it.

Yet another way that this book is different is in some of the tools it uses to explore issues surrounding measurement. Some tools used in this book are borrowed from economics, and if you are not an economist you may not have seen them before. I use them because they add value to the discussion by drawing attention to aspects of measurement situations (especially costs) that get left out of many analyses. As these tools are introduced, I explain them, provide advice on how to interpret them, and try to point out their implicit limitations.

Three Central Questions

Three questions are at the heart of this book:

1. How should measurement be used to improve the efficiency and effectiveness of organizations?

2. Why do real organizations often use measurement inappropriately, thereby causing measurement programs to fail or do harm?

3. What are the practical implications of the answers to the first two questions?

To answer these questions, I've taken three approaches.

First, I've conducted an extensive review of written materials related to measurement and performance management in fields ranging from economics to management theory to statistics to theater. By drawing on so many fields, we can make use of the special insights available in each. The many references to other source materials in this book, and its extensive bibliography, should assist any reader in search of more information on the subject.[1]

Second, I've constructed a model similar to models used by some economists. The model is a way of capturing the pattern of dysfunction, a mechanism that allows us to vary aspects of a measurement situation and see what happens. As such, it is a way to determine which situations make success possible and which situations make failure inevitable. Answers to central questions are derived primarily from the model.

Third, I've conducted interviews with eight people who are recognized experts in the use of measurement to manage a particular organizational activity: computer software development. The

---

[1] Where I've embedded references in the text, I list the foremost authorities first and then revert to chronological order.

content of expert interviews adds richness to this book's recommendations and explanations. The interviews also provide a check on assertions about the current state of thinking about measurement; the check is especially important at points where allegedly common ways of thinking are shown to contain flaws or contradictions. In addition, the interviews permit discovery of expert beliefs that are consistent with the model's explanations of measurement failure—alarmingly, the seeds of failure seem present in the advice of some experts.

My use of the word "expert" in this book is deliberate, but the word should be interpreted in a specific sense. I call these eight people experts because they are recognized repositories of state-of-the-art knowledge about software measurement—not because they agree with me (some of them don't). The fact that some experts' answers contain elements consistent with what I call a dysfunctional pattern does not mean that they are not experts, or that they cannot add value to a discussion of organizational measurement. So, throughout this book, I use quotes from all of the interviews to help me make points. I see no necessary contradiction or double standard in using the opinions of experts with whom I disagree on some points to make points on which we agree.

Who are these experts? Those who agreed to be identified are

- David N. Card, Software Productivity Solutions

- Tom DeMarco, Atlantic Systems Guild

- Capers Jones, Software Productivity Research

- John D. Musa, AT&T Bell Laboratories

- Daniel J. Paulish, Siemens Corporate Research

- Lawrence H. Putnam, Quantitative Software Management

- E.O. Tilford, Sr., Fissure

One expert wished to remain anonymous and is labeled Expert X when cited or discussed in this book. Names of experts are used throughout except in Chapter Sixteen, where expert answers to specific questions are analyzed and directly compared. Names are omitted in that chapter to prevent the appearance of ranking of experts, which is *not* one of the aims of this book.

Students of software measurement will recognize most, if not all, of these names. People who are less familiar with these experts may wish to know that this group, on average, has produced extensive book, periodical, and conference proceedings publications specifically on the subject of software measurement. Their experience in the software field ranges from fifteen to thirty years, and all have spent much of their careers working on measurement or related issues. These experts are a subset of all such experts in the world, but they are a relatively large subset in this new field. I estimate that there are no more than twenty other experts in the world who would be regarded by most practitioners as being on a par with these.

A Strategy for Reading This Book

Readers of this book will no doubt share an interest in organizational measurement as a management tool. But their deeper motivations may vary. Some will be interested because they need information they can use to improve the performance in their own organization; such readers may be rushing to satisfy specific needs for solutions that work right now. Other readers will be attracted by a general desire for understanding of organizational phenomena; these readers may be less hurried and may value more leisurely exposition and more detailed explanations. Where a reader falls on the spectrum between specific and general interest will influence what he or she gets out of each of the chapters of this book. I encourage you to think about where you fit on this spectrum, and, depending on what you decide, to vary your approach to reading this book. I have advice on how to vary your approach, but first I need to explain how the book is arranged.

This book is organized into nineteen chapters. Chapters One through Three introduce measurement issues, especially issues that surround measurement failure. Chapters Four through Nine directly address the first of the big questions highlighted above by constructing the model that is central to this book's treatment of measurement in organizations. Chapters Ten through Thirteen address alternative forms of management and some practical conclusions of the model about management styles and the organization of work. Chapters Fourteen through Sixteen turn to the second big question by extending the model to consider why measurement dysfunction arises and persists. Chapters Seventeen and Eighteen explore broader implications of the previous chapters' conclusions. And, finally, in Chapter Nineteen, an epilogue provides some summary thoughts on the book as a whole.

My advice on how to read this book is quite simple. For deepest understanding, read all of the chapters in detail. For a quicker tour with a more practical focus, skim Chapters Four through Eight (which present the details of the model used in this book), and carefully read Chapter Nine (a recap of Chapters Four through Eight). If you are especially pressed for time, read Chapters One through Three ("An Introduction to Measurement Issues," "A Closer Look at Measurement Dysfunction," and "The Intended Uses of Measurement in Organizations"), Chapter Seventeen ("The Measurement Disease"), and the concluding chapter. I suggest this last, very brief route through the book, in part, because I think it will suffice to hook you—to bring you back to the book at a later date, when you have more time available for reading.

What This Book Is Not About

This book does not deal with all important measurement-related issues. As I noted earlier, there is little here on the technical aspects of measuring, analyzing, or graphing specific measurements. Perhaps the most significant topic not addressed here, however, has to do with a moral dimension of the measurement problem. Aside from considerations of efficiency, feasibility, and cost, there are situations in which measurement is not appropriate for ethical reasons. Philosophical questions concerning privacy, fairness, and the like could be addressed in a book on measurement in organizations. But treating these issues adequately would require many more pages. My decision to exclude the bulk of moral issues from this book reflects my desire to treat capably a manageable slice of the measurement subject; it is not an indicator of how important I believe ethical issues to be.

To people who are interested in the moral aspects of measurement in organizations, I am pleased to report that by the end of this book I have established a case for the importance of ethical behavior purely on efficiency grounds. I show that ethical behavior should be practiced in many organizational contexts not because such behavior makes the world a better place (although that is also a fine reason) but because ethical behavior makes things work better. If there is a single message that comes from this book, it is that trust, honesty, and good intention are more efficient in many social contexts than verification, guile, and self-interest. To some, this conclusion may not seem profound. In my view, questions of the appropriate mixture of selfish individualism and selfless cooperation in a civilized society and its institutions are both profound and of the greatest practical importance.

June 1996   R.D.A.
London, England

MEASURING AND MANAGING
PERFORMANCE IN
ORGANIZATIONS

Chapter One:

An Introduction to
Measurement Issues

harles Schwab, the first president of Bethlehem Steel, liked to tour his steel-making plant daily. During one inspection he came on a group of employees who had just finished pouring ingot. Schwab quickly counted the ingot and without saying anything wrote "78" in bold figures on the hearth with a piece of chalk. Then he continued his tour. When he came to the same station a day later "78" had been crossed through, and beside it his employees had written "80." One day later, "80" was crossed out in favor of "85." Production continued to increase in this manner (Mason and Swanson, 1981, p. 224).

Stories like this are told in management circles to show how measurement can be used to improve organizational performance. The moral of the story: The simple act of measuring focused workers' attention on an important dimension of their performance and caused them to try to excel on that dimension. The result was increased output. Measurement apparently proved worthwhile. But compare this account with another in which the value of measurement is not so apparent: As the end of the 1968 fiscal year approached, Trans World Airlines (TWA) was headed for a major financial loss after recording sizable profits in 1967. In response to the crisis, TWA's managers took action: They "extended the depreciable life of most of [the airline] fleet by several years and took down more of [the] available investment tax credit in computing deferred income taxes" (Mason and Swanson, 1981, p. 137). When the ink was dry, TWA had gone from a near certain substantial loss to a profit equal to more than half of that of the previous year. Managers whose pay was based on the company's annual profit appreciated the change more than financial analysts trying to evaluate the health of the firm.

As in the first example, measurement at TWA caused employees to focus on a particular dimension of performance and to try to excel in performance on that dimension. The result was, as before, an increase in the magnitude of the measurement—profits increased. But few would argue that TWA's managers improved performance in any true sense. In terms of the true mission of the business enterprise, time spent devising such changes in accounting methods is wasted. Also, the changes reduced the usefulness of measurements to outsiders, including most stockholders, by creating ambiguity about what TWA profit measurements meant. The possibility of this kind of corruption of measures creates doubts that extend to all measurements. Were Bethlehem Steel employees making ingot smaller or lower in quality in their haste to impress Charles Schwab? Is there any real difference between the two scenarios other than the way they are perceived?

The importance of these two questions is revealed, in part, by observation of the extent of measurement use in organizations. Business firms measure profits, costs, financial and material flows, individual and group performance, and numerous other quantities. Government agencies measure compliance with laws and regulations, effectiveness of programs, demographic variation, and many of the same aspects of performance that concern business firms. A need for better understanding is revealed also by the surprising lack of consensus among management experts and practitioners. Disparities in claims about how measurement works, its usefulness, and appropriate uses are common.

Measurement is viewed by one influential group of management experts as necessary and extremely beneficial. David Garvin, writing in the *Harvard Business Review* (*HBR*), notes that managers believe that "if you can't measure it, you can't manage it" (July-August 1993, p. 78), a claim with which Garvin agrees; he argues that measured improvements are the only proof of useful learning by an organization. Others writing in the *HBR* also profess the virtues of measurement programs. Robert Kaplan and David Norton (January-February 1992, p. 71) recommend "a balanced scorecard" that "tracks the key elements of a company's strategy." Robert Eccles (January-February 1991, p. 131) maintains that "enhanced competitiveness depends on starting from scratch and asking: 'Given our strategy, what are the most important measures of performance?'" Bruce Chew (January-February 1988, p. 110) stresses the importance of measuring in his "No-Nonsense Guide to Measuring Productivity." Purveyors of management philosophies in many other venues portray measurement as a crucial part of effective business solutions. *The Economist* notes the prominence of measurement in popular business conceptions:

> [Corporate leaders] want to replace corporate bureaucracies with autonomous business units whose financial performance can be measured accurately by a tiny headquarters staff. . . . This trend draws on the work of innumerable management thinkers, who champion the idea of cutting corporate flab and "empowering" teams of employees, which can then be judged by their [measured] performance ("The Death of Corporate Loyalty," *The Economist*, April 3, 1993, p. 63).

Consistent throughout favorable treatments of measurement is acceptance as a first principle that measurement is a constructive practice that requires little or no justification. A story told by one software measurement expert in an interview for this study reveals a common attitude concerning the need (that is, lack of need) to justify measurement:

> I was in a meeting last week . . . and a woman in that meeting—she was a program manager—said, "Do you have any papers that discuss return on investment of software measurement programs?" . . . *I just sort of looked at her.* I said, "Well, no, but—it doesn't matter if this is software we are talking about or anything else we are talking about. . . . How is it that you have insight into how your programs are going?

> Is something on schedule? . . . How are we doing
> with respect to baselines or budgets or schedules? . . .
> How big is something?" . . . Whatever you are doing,
> you want some quantification of the[se] things . . .
> [emphasis added] (Expert X).

The question "Why quantify?" is not seriously addressed. Instead, a rhetorical parry suggests that the reason for measuring is obvious. Dan Paulish, another authority on software measurement interviewed for this study, stated that there is little downside risk for an organization using measurement properly, that the main challenge is in overcoming the resistance to measurement by organization members. Paulish and Expert X advance a line of reasoning adhered to by the many practitioners and academics who claim there is undeniable value to be obtained from measurement in almost any organizational setting, but that successful use hinges on "doing it right."

At a conceptual level, the benefits of measurement seem obvious. By holding workers accountable for their performance, as judged by a system of measurement, good workers can be rewarded and bad workers punished (for example, dismissed). Those who believe that they will be rewarded when they perform well are motivated to improve continuously. The best succeed and advance to positions of greater responsibility; the worst quit because most of the rewards are going to strong performers. The reward system is open and fair because performance criteria are unambiguous; meritocracy prevails.

The conceptual attractiveness of the measurement tool is reinforced by empirical findings in the psychological literature on goal setting that attest to communicative and attention-focusing effects of measurement. (See Latham and Locke, 1980, for a survey on this topic.) Furthermore, it can be reasonably argued that measurement is the only way to know what is really happening in an organization. The complexity of organizational processes hinders managers' attempts to interpret what they see happening. Only by taking fine-grained measurements at each stage of a complex process, in the manner of the careful experimentalist, can problems be discovered, pinpointed, and understood. Where improvement is attempted, only quantified assessments can provide unbiased, incontrovertible proof of progress.

A contrasting school of thought disputes the validity of the idealized conception of measurement put forth by measurement proponents. Measurement detractors stress the costs and potential for dysfunction associated with measurement in organizations. They recount stories of workers abusing machinery to meet production quotas and salespeople prevaricating on product features to meet sales targets. There are widely cited accounts of famous but unnamed Soviet boot and nail factories. The boot factories produced only size-7-left boots but never missed a production quota; the nail factories made a large number of small nails in response to numerical targets but switched skillfully to a small number of very large nails when targets were set by weight. Consistent with these anecdotes, Tom DeMarco, in an interview for this study, often referred to the "enormous cost" of measuring, in terms of the overhead necessary to maintain measurement mechanisms and the potential for less than constructive responses to measurement. Regarding the use of measurement to motivate people (as portrayed favorably in the Charles Schwab example), he said:

> In my experience, absolutely everybody who does it, screws it up. So I think the concept's wrong. And I think it's kind of pointless to think, "Well, if they did it right, it would be okay." They don't do it right. The people who want to do it are inclined to do it wrong.

Both the substance and the tone of these comments are at odds with more optimistic accounts of the impacts of measurement. In a similar vein, W. Edwards Deming, often considered father of both the Japanese and the American quality movements, has declared performance measurement "the most powerful inhibitor to quality and productivity in the Western world" (Gabor, 1989, p. 43). Such decided differences of opinion among experts is surely symptomatic of the need for further study.

The subtle nature of the differences between allegedly constructive and unconstructive uses of measurement can be illustrated by comparing examples of each. Consider V.F. Ridgway's (1956) account of a dysfunctional measurement system in use at an employment office that was first described by Blau in 1955 (see Blau, 2nd ed., 1963).

> . . . to stress the qualitative aspects of the [employment] interviewer's job, several ratios (of referrals to interviews, placements to interviews, and placements to referrals) were devised. Altogether, there were eight quantities that were counted or calculated for each interviewer (Ridgway, p. 243).

The ultimate dysfunction in this system rose from the interviewers' efforts to undermine the ratio indicators. For example, to inflate their placements-to-interviews ratio, interviewers destroyed records of interviews that did not result in placements (Blau, 1963). Now, compare Ridgway's account with Chew's (1988) description of what he considers an exemplary system in place in a major corporation more than thirty years later:

> A department develops several performance ratios (no fewer than three, no more than seven) that it believes capture the essence of its mission. For example, one design engineering team proposes six ratios, among which are: reworked drawings as a percentage of total drawings, overdue drawings as a percentage of total drawings, and overtime hours as a percentage of total hours (p. 114).

The similarities between the two programs, one offered as an example of dysfunction and the other as an example of an ideal, are striking. If the employment agents sought to invalidate their ratios, why don't design teams? On the other hand, if the design team system works, couldn't the employment office system be made to work?

There are differences between the two examples. Most obvious is that individual performance is being measured in the Ridgway example, while departmental performance is the focus in the Chew example. But it is not immediately apparent why this difference should account for the divergence in functionality of the two schemes. Members of a department do stand to gain from colluding to subvert departmental measures (being part of a seemingly successful team rarely damages team member prospects); and department members working jointly are probably *more* capable of devising means of measurement subversion than individuals. Furthermore, team measures are often attributed to the team's leader, thus becoming individual measures of a sort. Another difference (not apparent from the cited passages) is that Ridgway's indicators are used separately while Chew's indicators are combined into a single measure. Why this should matter also requires explanation. Perhaps there was also a difference in the degree to which people being measured were involved in the definition of measures. It is difficult to determine from the accounts provided. And there are probably other contrasts that would become apparent on close comparison of the two schemes. Which of the differences would make or break the system's functionality?

One troubling possibility is that one person's functional system is another person's dysfunctional system—that the difference is solely in the eye of the beholder. A contrast in the attitudes of Ridgway and Chew toward measurement is evident in their conclusions. Ridgway concludes that "quantitative performance measurements—whether single, multiple, or composite . . . have undesirable consequences for overall organizational performance" (p. 247). After discussing the same problems dealt with by Ridgway, Chew concludes that performance measures are nevertheless indispensable management tools. Such pronounced differences of opinion can be traced, at least in part, to differences in behavioral assumptions, in beliefs about what motivates people to work. Someone who believes that people always tend to avoid work might allow that measurement can be dysfunctional but might see no alternative to linking reward with performance in some way. At the opposite extreme, someone who believes that high levels of performance can only be motivated from within might see measurement as peripheral, entirely optional, and potentially distracting. Between these two extremes there is room for a variety of differing perspectives on measurement.

The length of time between the Ridgway and the Chew accounts—more than thirty years—attests to the durability of measurement issues. Eccles (1991) notes that General Electric began working to determine "key" performance measures in 1951 and that forty years later the measures generally used are not satisfactory. "The question that must be asked," venture Eccles and coauthor Philip Pyburn (1992), "is why it has been so difficult to do something that seems so obvious—create a more comprehensive system of performance measurement that combines financial and nonfinancial measures in the right proportion and in the right way?" (p. 42). The more pessimistic perspective of Ridgway yields equally puzzling questions: Why has measurement continued to be so widely used if it is such a destructive practice? Shouldn't some organizations have discovered error in their ways? And if so, shouldn't superior practices be propagated across the organizational landscape, whether by learning or selection?

In the current business climate, discouraging words about measurement are scarcely heard above clamorous approbation. But doubts linger. Managers convinced by assertions of measurement's benefits also recognize truth in tales of dysfunction. It seems reasonable, then, to study examples of dysfunction in search of a pattern, to determine how dysfunction operates, and how general the problem is. Detractors claim that the tendency of measurement systems to yield dysfunctional consequences is a danger to all who attempt measurement in organizations. Such claims can be evaluated only by gaining understanding of how common features of organizational situations contribute to dysfunction.

Research on measurement and dysfunction in organizations has historically proceeded along two main paths, with little interaction. Behavioral scientists, such as Ridgway and Peter Blau, have devoted considerable effort to the study of instances of dysfunctional measurement in organizations. A. Hopwood (1974) has noted of this body of work, however, that "surprisingly little consideration has been given to studying the precise determinants" and that the "approach has been pathological rather than diagnostic" (p. 103). The *economic theory of agency* (discussed in Chapter Four) follows an arguably more diagnostic line of research into measurement issues. But the real-world relevance of the agency literature's conclusions can be questioned because of the sacrifices it makes to maintain mathematical rigor. Features of organizational settings considered important by behavioral scientists and real managers (such as the internal motivations of workers) are excluded from nearly all economic theories of agency. Consequently, there is a need for a diagnostic understanding that is based on premises acceptable to behavioral scientists.

This book pulls together different lines of research and the experiences of real-world managers. It derives recommendations concerning the use of measurement in organizations and explains the persistence of dysfunction. It also examines the shared characteristics of organizational settings in which dysfunction occurs.

Chapter Two:

A Closer Look at
Measurement Dysfunction

B lau (1963) defines dysfunction broadly as "those observed consequences of social patterns that change existing conditions in the direction opposite to socially valued objectives, or consequences that interfere with the attainment of valued objectives" (p. 10). In an organizational context, dysfunction can be defined as consequences of organizational actions that interfere with attainment of the spirit of stated intentions of the organization. That dysfunction is violation of the spirit and not the letter of stated intentions is important. In the TWA case, managers increased profits, thus fulfilling a stated intention of their organization—but the way that TWA increased profits was not what the authors of those statements of intention meant.

Dysfunction's defining characteristic is that the actions leading to it fulfill the letter but not the spirit of stated intentions. There is, then, always some difficulty in creating a practical definition of dysfunction, especially for the purpose of preventing it. In a sense, TWA managers did exactly what was asked of them; it was those who set performance criteria who made the mistake, who asked for the wrong thing. It cannot be argued that TWA managers did not perform according to their contract, because they fulfilled it exactly as it was stated. Although the problem of practical definition often makes it hard to act against those who disseminate dysfunction, there is no practical difficulty in identifying instances of it.

Blau's (1963) famous employment office remains one of the best documented instances of dysfunctional measurement in an organizational setting. The government office had the stated purpose "to serve workers seeking employment and employers seeking workers." Early in the study period, employment interviewers were evaluated primarily by the number of interviews they conducted. Blau describes the dysfunctional result:

> Except for the information provided by direct observation, the number of interviews completed by the subordinate was the only evidence the supervisor had at that time for evaluating him. The interviewer's interest in a good rating demanded that he maximize the number of interviews and therefore prohibited spending much time on locating jobs for clients. This rudimentary statistical record interfered with the agency's objective of finding jobs for clients in a period of job scarcity (p. 38).

When office managers discovered that few placements were being made, they replaced the single indicator of performance with eight indicators. Improved agency performance seemed to follow. But a replication of Blau's study a few years later showed that much of what had seemed like improvement could be explained by more sophisticated dysfunctional behaviors. For example, to improve their showing on the indicator "percentage of interviews that resulted in job referrals," employment agents "engaged in outright falsification . . . by destroying at the end of the day those interviewing slips that indicated that no referrals to jobs had taken place" (p. 50). Blau summarized findings by remarking that

> . . . aside from such explicit deception, many of the activities of interviewers were oriented not so much to furnishing service as to improving the record. Thus, some clients were referred to jobs for which they were ill suited in endeavors to increase the number of referrals. The number of placements was

> even more important, and several [dysfunctional]
> devices were used to raise this figure (p. 50).

Attempts to eliminate the sources of dysfunction by introducing still more indicators failed because supervisors regarded the large number of indicators as too complex to provide a clear account of performance and therefore relied on a much smaller number of "key measures." The use of key measures led to dysfunctional behaviors in which employees directed their efforts to improving key measures at the expense of non-key measures (which became "more key" as performance slipped in those areas).

Defense procurement is a rich source of examples of dysfunctional measurement in interorganizational arrangements. A spectacular case resulted in the cancellation of the U.S. Navy's multi-billion dollar A-12 attack plane program. Then-Secretary of Defense Richard Cheney ended the program in January of 1991 after being told that it was behind schedule, overweight, and would cost an additional $2.7 billion to finish development (*The Economist*, January 12, 1991). The news came as an unwelcome surprise since Cheney had been told six months earlier that the program was on schedule and under budget. A formal inquiry traced the problem to management controls under which members of the development team worked. The inquiry report found that

> Notwithstanding the consistently negative trend of
> the cost and schedule performance data, the [con-
> tractor development] team continually made best
> case projections of cost at completion based upon
> overly optimistic recovery plans and schedule
> assumptions. The evidence indicated that the con-
> tractor team perceived significant pressure from
> upper management . . . to maximize cash flow. Such
> pressure would create an incentive to be optimistic,
> inasmuch as progress payments would be subject to
> reduction in the event of a contractor or Government
> estimate of an overrun (Beach, 1990, p. 5).

Such scenarios, in which program managers or contractors attend to measurements of *timeliness of delivery* to the exclusion of all else, are reported as early as 1882. In that year, the newly built U.S.S. *Omaha* was discovered to have onboard-coal-room for only four days' steaming; in the rush to stay on schedule, no one had been willing to force notice of this defect at a high enough level to ensure its correction. According to a report at the time, the *Omaha*'s "rebuilding cost the full price of an up-to-date steel ship, and [it] could neither fight nor run away from any contemporary ship of a foreign nation" (White, 1958, pp. 164-65).

Yet another example of dysfunctional measurement has engendered recent attempts to reform U.S. produce standards. Administered by the Department of Agriculture, the standards certify, for example, that a "U.S. Fancy broccoli stalk" has a diameter of not less than $2\frac{1}{2}$ inches, or that the color of a Grade A canned tomato is at least 90 percent "U.S.D.A. Tomato Red." The standards were originally devised to give the produce industry a common language to use in buying and selling fresh produce over phone lines and to ensure quality and safety of the produce that reaches the market. Reform proposals argue that there is growing evidence that the standards no longer guarantee quality and safety. In fact, because the standards are based almost entirely on the physical appearance of the produce, they encourage use of potentially dangerous pesticides. A 1989 E.P.A. draft report stated that many of "these applications [of pesticides] do not increase yields but simply serve the purpose of maintaining cosmetic appearance of fruits and vegetables from minute defects, such as surface scarring or blemishes, or slight amounts of insect fragments" (Sugarman, 1990, p. E1). The irony here, as in the previous two cases, is that the measured standards have actually interfered with the achievement of their intended effect.

There are countless documented examples of dysfunctional measurement within the criminal justice system. Blau (1963) describes dysfunctional effects of measurement in a federal law enforcement agency: Agents with case quotas tended to work easy-to-solve cases first, often neglecting bigger and more important cases. J. Skolnick (1966) demonstrates the corrupting effects of evaluating police departments by "clearance rates" (that is, the proportion of crimes solved), which are easily inflated by not recording some citizens' complaints, or by waiting to post them until the crime has been solved. Don Campbell (1979) summarizes the findings of researchers into a claim that former President Nixon's crackdown on crime "had as its main effect the corruption of crime-rate indicators."

Similar phenomena are reported in such diverse areas as public education, Soviet industrial administration, business administration, and warfare:

○ Primary- and secondary-school teachers being evaluated via pupils' performance on standardized tests tailor their instruction to the content of the tests. The resulting education of students is often narrower than is considered desirable by community and education leaders (see Hannaway, 1991; Stake, 1971).

○ Measuring the output of Soviet industrial plants caused abuses of machinery and a problem called "storming." Machines run at full tilt during the last half of a month in order to meet production targets invariably needed downtime during the first part of the next month. The downtime necessitated full-tilt running again for the second half of the month, which in turn necessitated more downtime. Goods "stormed" through the economy in dramatic fits and starts that severely strained industrial and transportation resources.

○ The State of California threatened to close all Sears automobile service centers because of allegations that Sears' sales commission system caused employees to charge customers for repairs that were not needed or not done (Fisher, 1992). Similar allegations were made in New Jersey. Sears eventually admitted, in an open letter to its customers published in major newspapers, that "our incentive and goal-setting program inadvertently created an environment in which mistakes have occurred" (Brennan, 1992).

○ It is considered axiomatic by business commentators that common measures of business performance, such as quarterly profits or stock value, often distort the incentives of U.S. business managers by emphasizing short-term over long-term objectives (Porter, 1992).

○ During the Vietnam War, the U.S. Department of Defense adopted a highly quantitative approach that used body counts, killed-by-air counts, kill ratios, and other measures to determine progress in the war and to evaluate strategies and operational units. The result was a multitude of dysfunctional behaviors. Field officers, concerned that measures would reflect on their individual performance, carefully managed what they reported, often inflating counts. It has even been suggested that a now-famous incident at My Lai in which a U.S. officer ordered the execution of hundreds of civilians was caused, in part at least, by this system of warfare management that pressured field units to raise their body counts (Campbell, 1979).

There is a clear pattern in these instances of dysfunction (see Fig. 2.1). When a measurement system is put in place, performance measures begin to increase. At first, the true value of an organization's output may also increase. This happens in part because workers do not understand the measurement system very well early on, so their safest course is to strive to fulfill the spirit of the system architects' intentions. Real improvement may result as well, because early targets are modest and do not drive workers into taking severe shortcuts. Over time, however, as the organization demands ever greater performance measurements, by increasing explicit quotas or inducing competition between coworkers, ways of increasing measures that are not consistent with the spirit of intentions are used. Once one group of workers sees another group cutting corners, the "slower" group feels pressure to imitate. Gradually, measures fall (or, more accurately, are pushed) out of synchronization with true performance, as workers succumb to pressures to take shortcuts. Measured performance trends upward; true performance declines sharply. In this way, the measurement system becomes dysfunctional.

It is important to understand what common features of the examples allow the pattern of dysfunction to unfold. It is important, also, to discover whether certain features lead inevitably to dysfunction, and whether those features can be altered in a way that does not upset the goals of a measurement system. Discovering and dissecting features that lead to dysfunction should provide insights into why dysfunction tends to recur and persist.

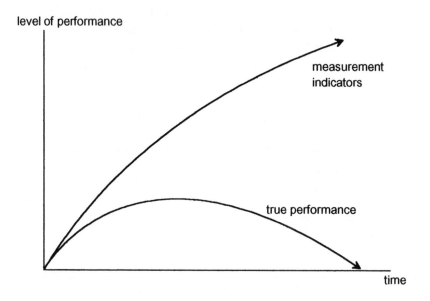

Figure 2.1: How dysfunction unfolds.

One feature common to all of the examples is that the indices used to measure are not perfectly related to the phenomena they purport to measure (Blau, 1963). Consequently, as Steven Kerr (1975) has noted, performance measurement systems frequently "reward A while hoping for B" (see Cummings and Dunham, p. 459). It is tempting to discount the seriousness of the problem by attributing it to this imperfection. Dysfunction, it might be argued, arises because a system measures too few things or the wrong things. The solution to the problem, then, would be more or better measures; the implication is that design of a dysfunctional system is faulty because it fails to measure important aspects of performance. There are, in fact, many advocates of refined multiple criteria measurement to solve the incentive distortion problem (see, for example, Drucker, 1954; Campbell, 1979).

The Blau employment office experience suggests, however, that the problem of dysfunction cannot always be eliminated by redesign of the reward system. Attempts by office managers to refine and expand that system were constrained by the cognitive limitations of evaluators: "The [multiple criteria system] . . . was too complex to furnish a clear-cut focus for performance, with the result that several pieces of information it contained were disregarded and a few were singled out for special attention . . ." (Blau, 1963, p. 52). More seriously, the implementation of more sophisticated measures caused more sophisticated dysfunctional reactions. Similar findings appear in other accounts of dysfunction (see, for example, Ridgway, 1956; Ouchi, 1981). Systems are frequently redesigned in unsuccessful attempts to eliminate the dysfunction. Often, multiple criteria systems are attempted and found not to be panaceas. Observation of the pattern leads Ridgway (1956) and Douglas McGregor (1960) to conclude that no measurement system can be designed to preclude dysfunctional behaviors.

Careful consideration of the examples reveals that the imperfect relationship between indices and what they purport to measure is caused by a disparity in the ease with which the different dimensions of performance can be measured. Nobel laureate economist Ken Arrow (1971) describes the problem, as it pertains to business firms, in the following manner:

> . . . management must have a way of measuring performance. This may be the objective function itself, or it may be some other, *more easily measurable,* index. If the index is something other than the objective itself, the manager's incentives may not be directed optimally from the viewpoint of the corporation; for example, if the index of the manager's performance is based primarily on output rather than profits, he will be tempted to be wasteful of inputs [emphasis added] (p. 228).

The difficulty is that some of the characteristics of performance that the organization wishes to encourage may not be easily measurable, so measures cannot be made comprehensive enough to track everything of interest to organizational managers. Kaoru Ishikawa (1985), a Japanese quality control expert, provides an example of an unmeasurable "true quality characteristic" of newsprint rolls: the degree to which they resist tearing when printed on by a rotary press (see especially pp. 47-50). The only available test of this true characteristic is a destructive one—actually printing on the paper. So, in purchasing newsprint rolls, it is necessary to rely on substitute characteristics, like weight, thickness, and so on, which can be more easily measured. But, as Ishikawa points out, substitute characteristics are necessarily imperfect indicators of true characteristics; paper acceptable in weight and thickness may still be prone to tear on the printing press. Focusing on necessarily imperfect indices constitutes "*displacement of goals* whereby an instrumental value becomes a terminal value" (Merton, 1957). An important special case of reliance on imperfect measures occurs in performance measurement. Employees' *true output* (such as value to the organization) is often intangible and difficult to measure; in its place, organizations choose to measure inputs (such as the amount of effort devoted to the task as measured by counts of interviews performed).

Substitution of inputs for true output is justified in practice by observed correlations. For example, satisfaction with the activities of an employment office usually means that many interviews are occurring. Defense officials being pleased with an acquisition usually means that the product was delivered on time. Customers being happy with a tomato means it is more likely to be beautiful than blemished. The assumption is that strong performance implies that measures are in favorable ranges. But the implication rarely holds in both directions. A large number of interviews being achieved in an employment agency need not imply general satisfaction with its performance. On-time delivery does not guarantee satisfaction with a new airplane. Beautiful fruit might be shunned when unacceptable actions are taken to reduce surface scarring. Aristotle (335 B.C.) was surely among the first to record the human tendency to forget the directional nature of implication on observing correlation:

> . . . assuming that if one thing is or becomes, a second is or becomes, men imagine that, if the second is, the first likewise is or becomes. But this is a false inference . . . the mind, knowing the second to be true, falsely infers the truth of the first . . . (see Aristotle, in Dukore, ed., p. 52).

The conclusion is fallacious because when correlation is not a consequence of implication in both directions, the stability of the correlation need not persist.[1] And, as the examples have shown, it is often in the best interest of the people being measured to make certain that correlations assumed by designers of measurement systems do not persist. Employment agents, design team members, or whoever, can increase their rewards if they can successfully obliterate correlation between true output and measured performance.

Even when rewards are not intentionally associated with favorable performance, there can be dysfunctional effects. Consider the produce standards example. Suppose there were no provision for government inspection and grading of fruits and vegetables in current standards legislation, but instead, that farmers were asked to voluntarily comply with standards. Such an arrangement would leave curtailing of cheating on produce grading to the market (that is, farmers dishonest about the grade of their produce would have fewer repeat customers), but the standards themselves would still have value because the grades facilitate transactions. Rather than try to describe how red his tomatoes are, a farmer could simply use the U.S.D.A. designation, thereby making pricing of sight-unseen products easier. Used in this way, the standards have no *intended* evaluative function—they are intended solely to facilitate communication. Even in a case such as this one, though, the described dysfunction would

---

[1] This classic logical fallacy is commonly called "Affirming the Consequent."

be expected to arise, since better produce grades are naturally associated with higher profits for farmers. Even if cheating on grading were impossible, farmers would have incentives to use pesticides to make fruits and vegetables more attractive, despite the fact that the standards were not intended to evaluate. The standard would still focus evaluation of the worth of the produce on one dimension of its character—its external appearance. Similarly, in an organizational setting, an individual manager may feel that a measure has impact on his or her career "profitability," even if the measure were put in place for, say, planning reasons, to determine when more resources might need to be brought to bear on a project.

Chapter Three:
The Intended Uses of Measurement in Organizations

B ecause dysfunction is defined with respect to organizational intentions, any study of it must pay careful heed to exactly what is intended by measurement system architects. Intended uses of measurement can be partitioned into two categories:

o *Motivational measurements* are explicitly intended to affect the people who are being measured, to provoke greater expenditure of effort in pursuit of organizational goals.

o *Informational measurements* are valued primarily for the logistical, status, and research information they convey, which provides insights and allows better short-term management and long-term improvement of organizational processes.

The distinction between the two categories is sharpened by the observation that motivational measurement is, by definition, intended to cause reactions in the people being measured, while informational measurement should be careful *not* to change the actions of the people being measured. Informational measurement must be careful not to affect behavior, because the information conveyed by measures is likely to be most representative of actual events when people being measured behave as if the measurement system did not exist (Roesthlisberger and Dickson, 1939).

Whether measurement is intended to motivate or to provide information, or both, turns out to be very important. In some situations, the two categories of measurement become incompatible. Attempts to force compatibility cause dysfunction. Figuring out what makes measurement work as intended and what makes it fail or cause serious problems begins with a close look at the two categories of measurement.

Motivational Measurement

The motivational use of measurement is familiar to most people in its most overt forms, such as sales bonuses, incentive pay, merit pay, pay-for-performance, or any other attempt to reward strong performance monetarily as determined by an established measurement system. Systems that associate less tangible rewards, such as increased probability of promotion, with measured strong performance, operate on the same principle. Under these systems, people who produce measured outcomes in desirable ranges are rewarded; people who fail to perform according to measurements may be punished (for example, dismissed).

The recent trend is toward more explicit links between measured performance and reward. A 1988 report on executive compensation in financial institutions (Peat Marwick, 1988) revealed that 87 percent of the banks, thrifts, insurance companies, and diversified financial firms surveyed had incentive plans for their executives, compared with 82 percent in 1987. Fully 98 percent of banks used incentive plans. A more recent report by Hewitt Associates, a compensation consulting firm, showed that the number of U.S. companies offering variable pay to all salaried employees increased from 47 percent in 1988 to 68 percent in 1993 (Tully, 1993). Companies now pay more in incentive compensation than in salary increases. In 1993, bonuses and other incentive payments averaged 5.9 percent of base salary, compared with 3.9 percent five years earlier. By comparison, the average raise in 1993 was just 4.3 percent.

Viewed theoretically, motivational measurement is a means of encouraging compliance with prescribed plans of action. An organization establishes relationships with other organizations and with individuals to obtain resources and capabilities needed to execute its plans. These other organizations and individuals do not usually have an inherent interest in the successful execution of the first organization's plan, but they take an interest in exchange for help in meeting some of their own needs or to avoid a worsening of their condition that might be brought about by the first organization. In this way, a group composed of organizations and individuals is bound together by a network of *contracts*, commonly understood formal or informal agreements that specify what is to be done (or not done) or to be provided by each member of the group.[1] Through creation of the network of contracts, the goals of the group's founder are extended to the group as a whole. The contractual arrangements that bind them together can then be said to be *functional*, if they tend to produce results consistent with expressed goals, or *dysfunctional*, if they tend to produce results inconsistent with those goals.

Economists have traditionally regarded the contractual relationships that bind such groups together as simple exchanges. Terms of the agreement are specified initially; when both sides have met their terms, the contract is complete. Contracts may be entered into repeatedly; their specifications may be contingent on outcomes determined by nature (for example, "If it rains more than ten days in April, construction shall be completed by the end of May; otherwise, by May 15"); or they may extend over long periods of time. In each of these cases, functioning of the contract as a prespecified exchange is similar in principle to and little different from any other transaction in which goods are exchanged or purchased. However, as organizational theorists (see, for example, March and Simon, 1958; Pfeffer, 1990) and institutional economists (see Coase, 1937; Alchian and Demsetz, 1972; Williamson, 1975) have pointed out, some arrangements between

---

[1] In a slight departure from the usual use of the word "contract," this includes agreements in which one party does not enter freely, as, for example, when a government imposes a requirement on a business firm without consideration (for example, monetary payment).

cooperating parties pose challenges to the notion of a contract as a simple exchange.

The *employment contract*, for example, seems at odds with economists' idealizations. Chester Barnard's (1938) *inducements and contributions* framework, widely cited in explanations of the employment relationship, does have an economic flavor. Barnard argues that inducements given to each employee must exceed what the employee is asked to contribute or else cooperation will cease. The framework is clearly based on the notion of exchange but, in a departure from the usual economic portrayal of exchange, this transaction is not clearly defined or prespecified. The employee agrees not to specific terms, but rather to act in a general way on the employer's behalf, within the "zone of acceptance"[2] of the employee (March and Simon, 1958), in exchange for payment. Contract terms are not fully specified because neither employee nor employer knows in advance what will be required in pursuit of the employer's goal; the employee is expected to exercise discretion. In performing the job, the employee gains job-specific knowledge that the employer does not possess. The ambiguity of contract terms and the private job-knowledge of the employee make it hard for the employer to determine whether the employee is fulfilling his or her part of the contract. Therefore, the possibility of employee opportunism arises. The exchange between employee and employer becomes complicated as terms are ambiguous and verification of contract performance is difficult.

Contracts involved in cooperative work, whether formal employment contracts or another sort, often have verification of performance difficulties. Concerns that the opportunism of one member might undermine achievement of the group goal are common and legitimate. There is a need for the group's leader or leaders to exert influence over group members in a way that causes them to adhere to the spirit of their respective contracts;

---

[2] Barnard's actual phrase was "zone of indifference," which is not quite right. Employees have preferences even within their zone of *acceptance*. Preferences within the zone play an important part in explanations of some organizational phenomena (for example, dysfunction). Perhaps this is why James March and Herbert Simon prefer the word *acceptance*.

that is, there is a need for *control* of the group action. Motivational measurements and their associated incentive plans are a response to the need for control. By measuring a group member's performance and explicitly associating rewards with favorable measurements, the group member's incentives are, in theory, brought into alignment with those of the group's leader. The member works harder and in the way desired by the leader. Recall that previously described instances of dysfunction occurred when measurements were faulty, in that the alignment of interests produced was imperfect. Imperfect alignment may result in more effort being expended by employees but in the wrong way. Both the amount of effort expended and how the effort is allocated across task activities are important determinants of the eventual value of the work. In the Blau example, nothing of value can come of employment-agent activities if prospective employers are never contacted, regardless of how earnestly agents devote effort to interviewing prospective employees.

Informational Measurement

Informational measurement can take two different forms. The first, which might be called *process refinement measurement*, provides information that reveals the detailed structure of organizational processes. Detailed accounts of the internal workings of processes are useful in designing improved processes, thereby making the organization function more efficiently. Frederick Taylor (1916) pioneered this use of measurement. He proposed using organizational quasi-experiments to determine the laws and parameters governing production processes ("Every little trifle—there is nothing too small—becomes the subject of an experiment. . . ." p. 75). In an often cited example, he showed that more total weight could be loaded if a man did not lift his maximum load each time; lifting the maximum load each time reduced the overall rate at which he could lift, thereby reducing the total amount that could be lifted in a day. After Taylor's experiment, loaders of coal and iron ore were given strict orders concerning how much to lift in each shovel, and the result was more efficient loading. In a similar vein, Campbell (1979) proposed designing government social programs as quasi-experiments with built-in measurements.[3]

The second form of informational measurement, *coordination measurement*, has a purely logistical purpose. Coordination measurement provides information that allows short-term (sometimes real-time) management of organizational flows and schedules. For example, it benefits a print shop to measure its current stores and usage rates of various kinds of paper so that shortages or burdensome inventories can be avoided. Likewise, knowing how far ahead or behind schedule a software project is running can help managers avoid bringing resources to bear too early or too late. In rudimentary form, coordination measurement generates simple warnings or red flags, such as the light that flickers on a car dashboard indicating dangerously low oil levels.[4]

The informational use of measurement in its conceptually pure form is not intended to have motivating effects on workers. Its purpose, rather, is to learn about whatever is being studied or managed. A physicist reading from a voltmeter during a lab experiment is using measurement purely informationally. In such contexts of conceptual purity, measurement has been described as "the assignment of numerals to objects according to rules" (Stevens, 1946, p. 677), "assigning numbers to represent qualities" (Campbell, 1957, p. 267), and, more elaborately, "the establishment of empirical rules of correspondence between a set of empirical objects (A) and a set of numerals (N)" (Grove *et al.*, 1977, p. 220). An often repeated assertion by Lord Kelvin espouses the virtues of purely informational measurement:

> When you can measure what you are speaking
> about, and express it in numbers, you know some-
> thing about it; but when you cannot measure it,
> when you cannot express it in numbers, your knowl-

---

[3] Most experts interviewed for this study recommended such quasi-experimental uses of measurement. David Card described an informational research program in place in his organization that he believes has led to better understanding of processes involved in software production.

[4] Most experts interviewed for this study cited logistical coordination as a legitimate use of measurement.

> edge is of a meager and unsatisfactory kind; it may
> be the beginning of knowledge, but you have scarce-
> ly in your thoughts advanced to the stage of science
> (as quoted in Humphrey, 1989, pp. 3–4).

Proponents of organizational measurement take the claims expressed by Lord Kelvin deeply to heart. Some aspire to a science of organizational measurement; others place great practical store in the power of quantification to reveal aspects of the organizational world. Many posit analogies between measurement in physical and organizational systems. One frequent analogy casts the manager in the role of an airplane pilot guided by organizational measures that are like cockpit instruments. Kaplan and Norton (1992) use this analogy in their paper advocating multiple criteria measurement systems:

> Think of [the organizational measurement system] as
> the dials and indicators in an airplane cockpit. For
> the complex task of navigating and flying an air-
> plane, pilots need detailed information about many
> aspects of the flight. They need information about
> fuel, air speed, altitude, bearing, destination, and
> other indicators that summarize the current and pre-
> dicted environment (p. 72).

Several experts interviewed for this book repeated versions of this analogy. Capers Jones also made comparisons to medical diagnosis, stating that just as doctors seeking to explain a patient's ills measure blood pressure and pulse, so should managers seek out organizational ailments by checking flows, rates, and trends. Jones carried the comparison to the point of characterizing some measurement advice as "measurement malpractice."

Outside of the theoretical realm, however, it is nearly impossible to achieve the purity of informational measurement inherent in these analogies. Unlike mechanisms and organisms, organizations have subcomponents that realize they are being measured. Russell Ackoff (1971) draws a careful distinction between organisms and organizations (concisely paraphrased here by Mason and Swanson):

> . . . both are purposeful systems in the sense that each can change its goals. The difference is that organisms are comprised of organs that only serve the purpose of the system, whereas organizations are comprised of purposeful subsystems with their own goals (see Mason and Swanson, p. 135).

Organizational subsystems are composed of people, most of whom maintain among their goals the desire to look good in the eyes of those responsible for evaluating and allocating rewards to the subordinate subsystems. The desire to be viewed favorably provides an incentive for people being measured to tailor, supplement, repackage, and censor information that flows upward. Eric Flamholtz (1979) reacts to the extension of purist definitions of measurement into organizational contexts by protesting that

> In the context of organizations, the role of measurement is *not* merely a technical role of representation; it has social and psychological dimensions as well. The function of accounting measurement systems, for example, is not merely to represent the properties of "wealth" (measured in terms of "assets") and "income"; but rather to fulfill a complex set of functions. . . . Accounting measurements are *simultaneously* intended to facilitate the functions of accountability (stewardship), performance evaluation, and motivation, as well as provide information for decision making (Flamholtz, 1979. See also Mason and Swanson, p. 255).

Mechanistic and organic analogies are flawed because they are too simplistic. Kaplan and Norton's cockpit analogy would be more accurate if it included a multitude of tiny gremlins controlling wing flaps, fuel flow, and so on of a plane being buffeted by winds and generally struggling against nature, but with the gremlins always controlling information flow back to the cockpit instruments, for fear that the pilot might find gremlin replacements. It would not be surprising if airplanes guided this way occasionally flew into mountainsides when they seemed to be progressing smoothly toward their destinations.

Segregating Information By Intended Use

In the last few words of his above protest, Flamholtz (1979) notes that measurements are intended to provide a basis for decision making. This is true of all measurement categories. Motivational measurement is used to decide whom to reward and whom to punish, thereby providing impetus for workers. Refinement of process measurement is used to decide which processes to redesign and how to redesign them. Coordination measurement is used to decide when to acquire new resources and how to allocate them.

It is important to notice that the distinctions between the categories of measurement reside entirely in distinctions between the categories of the decisions for which they are intended to provide information. Nothing about a piece of information makes it inherently motivational or informational. Rather, it is the way in which the information is used that determines the measurement category. Measuring the progress of a software project and comparing the measurements against planned progress generates information that is probably of interest to someone. But knowing the nature of the information and how it is generated does not permit categorization of the measurement. Something more must be known about the way in which the information will be used. If the reason for measuring is to decide who among project managers should receive the largest salary increase, then the measurement is motivational. If the reason for measuring is to decide how to improve development processes, then the measurement is process refinement. And if the reason for measuring is to decide when more resources should be added to the project, then the measurement is coordination.

Because the category of measurement is not inherent in the information provided by the measurement, information is difficult to segregate by intended use. Difficulty in segregating information yields a consequent difficulty in dictating how measurement information will be used. Information on whether a project is behind schedule can be used either motivationally or informationally, regardless of what was intended when the measurement system was put in place. The designers of a measurement system are usually powerless to guarantee that measurement information will be used in accord with their intentions, if not from the moment of the installation then certainly by the time the system has been in place for a while.

People working on activities that are being measured understand that dictating the uses of measurement is difficult and choose their behaviors accordingly. Unless trust between workers and managers is greater than usual in organizations, claims that measurement will only be used in a particular way are not credible. Regardless of official declarations, workers may believe it is in their interest to assume that available information will be used for performance evaluation and begin preparing for that possibility. In preparing for motivational measurement, people being measured will glean information from the design of the measurement system. Ridgway (1956) points out that

> Even where performance measures are instituted purely for purposes of information, they are probably interpreted as definitions of the important aspects of that job or activity and hence have important implications for the motivation of behavior (p. 247).

People in organizations have a justifiable interest in understanding what is important to those who make decisions about rewards and punishments. And measurement systems—even those that are supposed to be purely informational—provide some of this understanding.

As has been shown in the examples, dysfunction is a possible result of the difficulty in segregating uses of information. Dysfunction occurs when the validity of information delivered by a system of measurement is compromised by the unintended reactions of those being measured. Unintended reactions become possible whenever measures are imperfect. Recall the hypothetical farm-produce regulation example at the end of Chapter Two; produce ratings were not intended to be evaluative, but, rather, to provide a common language for use by buyers and sellers in talking about fruits and vegetables over telephone lines. The intention of the regulation is coordination, to allow buyers to make purchases based on independently verified grade rather than based on expensive trips to inspect produce being considered for purchase. The dysfunction arises in such a case because motivational uses of the measurement information are not precluded by the design of the measurement system. The price of some grades is higher, and buyers and farmers react to that fact, regardless of the system designers' intentions.

Note that many measurement systems are expressly intended to serve both motivational and informational purposes. It is common to hear motivational phrases like "improved accountability" intermingled with informational phrases like "better understanding of processes" in justifications of organizational measurement systems. As will be shown, even some experts have these dual expectations of their measurement systems. When systems are expected to perform motivationally *and* informationally, situational characteristics that affect the quality of measures become critical. For many such systems, the phenomena being measured seem far too complex to permit perfect measurement, which in turn seems to imply dire consequences for the systems' prospects of avoiding dysfunction. Unless the latitude to subvert measures can be eliminated (that is, unless measures can be made perfect)—a special case—or some means can be established for preventing certain kinds of information use (for example, if it could be made unthinkable within an organization's culture to use measurement to evaluate people), dysfunction seems destined to accompany organizational measurement. The sense of inevitability in Campbell's (1979) law of corruption of measurement indicators seems justified:

> The more any quantitative social indicator is used for social decision-making, the more subject it will be to corruption pressures and the more apt it will be to distort and corrupt the social processes it is intended to monitor (p. 85).

Chapter Four:

How Economists Approach the Measurement Problem

The link between management practice and research in economics is tenuous at best. One reason is that economists commonly use complex mathematics that are inaccessible to most nonspecialists. Another reason is that the assumptions underlying many economic models are so simplified that it is difficult to take them seriously as descriptions of real organizational situations. Despite these objections, however, there are ideas of interest imbedded within the mathematically rigorous yet drastically oversimplified models of economics. It is worth considering these ideas, without the technical detail, as a starting point for the analysis of motivational measurement.

Economists began to consider motivational measurement in depth as a result of papers by Steven Ross (1973) and Bengt Holmström (1979). Resulting from the Ross-Holmström (R-H) model is a voluminous literature that seeks to extend the economic approach to the internal workings of the firm and to consider how payments to employees should be arranged. There are many variations but the entire literature bears an obvious debt to the original formulation.

The R-H model portrays an organization in drastically simplified form, composed of only two people with interacting roles. The *principal* is the instigator of cooperative activity. She controls the facilities necessary to the venture and retains the right to allocate any consequent revenues.[1] The *agent* is hired by the principal to exert effort; he uses the facilities to do the actual revenue-producing work. In effect, the principal is a manager and the agent is an employee. The venture produces revenues that are shared by principal and agent, according to a rule determined in advance by the principal and known to the agent. Revenues kept by the principal are her profits. Revenues given to the agent are his payment for services.

The model also employs simple assumptions about motivation. The agent is motivated only by his fondness for money and his dislike of work. The principal cares only about profit, defined as the amount of the venture's revenues that she does not have to share with the agent. So, the agent and the principal have opposed interests. The principal wants as much effort as she can get from the agent in exchange for as little money as possible. The agent wants as much money as he can get in exchange for as little effort as possible.

How their interaction unfolds hinges on one of the model's central observations: *The agent's effort gets more expensive as its level increases*. If getting the agent to go from two units of effort to three units of effort costs a $5 increase in his wage, then going from three units to four units might cost a $7 increase. Going from four to five effort units would require an even greater increase for the agent—say, a $10 increase in wage. The intuition behind this observation is sensible: The harder the agent works, the more he is likely to demand for increasing his effort a little more. And the more he is paid, the less he values each additional dollar. Effort becomes more dear to the agent at the same time that money becomes less dear, as he simultaneously works harder and gets richer. So, it costs the principal more and more to get additional effort out of the agent.

A moment's reflection reveals that the increasingly expensive nature of agent effort is very important to the principal. She values additional agent effort because it raises the level of total revenues and creates the potential for greater profits. But the

---

[1] For clarity of exposition in this discussion, the principal will always be referred to by feminine pronouns and the agent by masculine pronouns.

amount of the revenues that will need to be shared with the agent also gets bigger as the level of effort increases. There is a point, then, beyond which agent effort becomes too expensive to profitably acquire. Increases in effort beyond this point *would* raise revenues—but the payment required by the agent would be greater than the increase in the revenues. So the profit-seeking principal should not try to increase effort beyond that point.

How should the principal set up a payment schedule for the agent that will obtain the right amount of effort—not too much and not too little? Consider a payment rule that says to the agent, "If your effort reaches level X, I will pay you $Y; otherwise, I will pay you nothing." Such an all-or-nothing arrangement is called a *forcing contract*, and there is much to recommend it. If the payment of Y dollars allows the agent at least slightly more satisfaction (economists use the word "utility") than he is able to obtain on the labor market at large, then he will comply exactly with the terms of the contract. The agent gains nothing by exerting less than the specified level of effort, because the principal pays him nothing for producing that effort; he gains no additional money by exceeding the specified level of effort and he *does* accrue additional effort displeasure (*dis*utility) for exceeding the specified level. The amount of the payment, Y, can be set by the principal so that it barely satisfies the agent's minimum utility requirement at the specified effort level, X. The amount of money needed to satisfy the agent increases with effort level and can be calculated for each level of effort. The principal can then compare the cost and revenues associated with each level of effort and choose the level of effort that maximizes her profits. This level of effort becomes the X in the optimal forcing contract and the required payment to the agent becomes the Y.

Balancing Cost and Benefit Associated with Agent Effort

The preceding story about balancing cost and benefit of additional agent effort underlies all motivational measurement models in the economics literature. The story is relevant to management practice because it accounts for costs that are sometimes overlooked in practice. Managers often fail to consider the increasing costs of additional effort from employees, especially when those cost increases are implicit, such as increases due to lower quality when employees work faster. Other costs that get left out of managers' mental accounting will be important later in this book, especially the costs of creating and maintaining a system to verify agent effort expenditures. The basic form of the cost-to-benefit argument recurs throughout this book and is worth summarizing for emphasis, as follows:

> The principal designs a system that links a reward with meeting an effort target. For the target to be meaningful, the reward must be enough to yield net satisfaction to the agent, or he may take his labor elsewhere. When the target is meaningful, the agent will meet it exactly. The cost of making the target meaningful to the agent is, then, a variable of primary concern to the principal. Meaningful targets at higher levels of effort bring benefit in the form of greater revenues, but they are also more costly. At some point, it becomes too expensive to get more effort out of the agent; targets set beyond this point require more in additional cost to make them meaningful than they produce in extra revenues. Design of the incentive system amounts to solving the problem of discovering the optimal point, at which marginal revenue and marginal cost just offset each other.

In fairness to the economics literature, it must be noted that an important detail has been omitted from the above discussion. In the R-H model, and others like it, agent effort is not directly observable. The principal can only determine the agent's effort level by looking at the level of revenues that result. Effort level does not map deterministically to a single revenue level. So, revenue level does not exactly reveal effort level. Increasing the level of agent effort *increases the likelihood* of higher revenues but it does not *guarantee* higher revenues. Thus, the relationship between effort and revenue is probabilistic rather than exact. The justification for this additional complication is twofold: 1) Managers cannot watch employees' effort expenditure all the time, so effort cannot be directly observed; and 2) a company's revenues are influenced by many things in addition to the effort level of employees, such as the state of the economy, so effort and revenue levels are not deterministically related.

This hazier relationship between unobserved effort and observed revenues may at first seem like a minor point, but it complicates the derivation of a payment schedule. Schedules can still be contingent on revenues in some manner because revenues signal the level of agent effort to the principal. But forcing contracts are no longer obviously appropriate since the agent cannot assure a given level of revenue. Actual revenue outcomes may fall above or below the expected level, due to factors beyond the agent's control. Depending on the agent's attitude toward risk, he may demand a considerable surcharge in exchange for taking on a job in which the potential revenue outcomes are partially beyond his control. Deriving a payment schedule for conditions in which effort and revenues are only related probabilistically requires some mathematical virtuosity that will not be reproduced here. The result of such a derivation *is* of interest, however: *The optimal payment schedule is one in which payment to the agent increases as revenues increase.* This result can be interpreted as a recommendation to design incentive systems in which rewards are increased as measured performance improves.

In other words, *this simple model, based on caricatures of the typical organization and individual motivation, produces a justification for common forms of merit pay, pay-for-performance, and motivational measurement schemes known by other names.* This conclusion should be both impressive and disturbing. It should be impressive as an intellectual achievement because such simple assumptions have borne predictions that match well with worldly practice. The conclusion should be disturbing because much of common practice seems based on drastic oversimplification. Surely, organizations are more complex than in this model's portrayal. Surely, employees care about more than making money and avoiding work. And surely, managers care about more than the bottom line. The conclusion also yields some food for thought: If you believe in pay-for-performance, consider whether your underlying opinions about organizations and individual motivation contain oversimplified notions such as those that underlie the R-H model.

The Effort Mix Problem

In the R-H model, effort levels are one-dimensional. The model deals entirely with magnitude of effort induced by an incentive schedule. It ignores the fact that most productive activity involves allocating effort across a number of tasks—deciding on a productive mix of effort across tasks. Good managers know that how smart employees work matters at least as much as how hard they work, especially in jobs that involve a lot of mental activity. Recall from Blau's employment office example that employees who were working very hard effectively undermined the organization's objectives by spending too much time interviewing job candidates and too little time making referrals. The problem facing the principal is how to arrange payment schedules to encourage appropriate magnitude and mix of effort by the agent.

Dysfunction arises when efforts to make the agent work harder cause him to shift effort from one dimension of his job to another in a way that produces a less-productive effort mix and reduces value to the customer. Interestingly, in examples of dysfunction, the principal seems to set payment schedules that cause bad behavior by the agent. The principal is usually harmed by the agent's bad behavior when customers become displeased. Why does the principal seemingly undermine her own success in this way?

Part of the answer comes from noticing that models based on only a single-effort dimension have nothing to say about dysfunction. The R-H model recommends that practitioners construct payment schedules that increase with measured performance. But just such payment schedules caused the dysfunction in the examples presented in Chapter Two. One begins to wonder if dysfunction appears in real settings because managers' mental models are too simple in the same ways that the R-H model is too simple.

The economists Holmström and Paul Milgrom (1991) turned their attention to the mix problem to consider a job composed of more than one task. The job has the property that if *no* effort is devoted to any one of the tasks, then *no* valuable output can result, just as in the Blau example. Also as in the Blau example (and many others), Holmström and Milgrom assume that at least one such task is completely unobservable, and that there is no signal of effort level for that task. They demonstrate that a payment schedule that increases in measured performance can cause the optimizing agent to divert all effort away from the unmeasured task to the measured task, thus producing no valuable output. They show also that as long as the agent is not strictly effort averse—that is, *as long as he finds it pleasurable to expend some effort that yields value to the customer*—the principal will prefer to pay a fixed fee that does not depend on measured performance. In the fixed-fee arrangement, the principal gets some value out of the agent, whereas the increasing-in-output payment schedule causes the agent to shift to a harmful mix of effort and thereby produce nothing of value.

Pleasurable effort outlays are not a part of most economic models. This break with tradition is important but not complete. Holmström and Milgrom do move in the direction of more sophisticated notions of motivation. But they do not ask some suggested next questions: Might agents be persuaded to enjoy doing more work that is beneficial to the principal, regardless of promises of monetary reward? Might internal motivation be called on to solve incentive problems? If so, how? Making workers more willing to work toward the goals of the company—by persuasion, by evoking feelings of identification with the firm, or by other methods—is an often-used mode of organizational control (Barnard, 1938; Ouchi, 1979). By not addressing internal motivation in more depth, Holmström and Milgrom ignore a part of motivation that is considered important by real managers and behavioral scientists.

Nevertheless, the Holmström and Milgrom (H-M) formulation contains innovations of considerable importance. First, the assumption that what is measured is a perfect indicator of the true value produced by the agent has been abandoned. The validity of the model is thereby greatly improved, since it is very difficult to find measures in real organizations that exactly represent the *true output* of production processes. R.J. Chambers (1960) has shown how "widely used business measurements are inadequate or invalid" as measures of true output. Measurements often do not represent what they purport to represent, and they are able to be manipulated by those with vested interests in their outcomes.

Even output measures such as revenues are vulnerable to manipulation by firm managers who can change accounting methods. Replacing the assumption that true output is measurable are the more realistic assumptions that 1) most jobs are composed of multiple tasks, 2) effort devoted to tasks is often signaled individually rather than collectively, and 3) signals are not available for effort devoted to some tasks. True output, which depends jointly on effort devoted to all tasks, is not available to be measured directly and cannot be the basis for payment schedules.

A related innovation of the H-M formulation is recognition that value is provided in a non-additive manner as agents devote effort to tasks. In the Blau employment agency example, value of the work done by agents is not equal to the simple sum of value from interviews and value from referral activities (such as calls to prospective employers). If value were additive, then value would be provided even when agents conducted many interviews but performed no referral activities. In fact, no value is provided by the agency without referral activities. In other words, referral is a *critical dimension* of effort expenditure. An effort dimension is critical when no valuable output can be created without devoting effort to the dimension.[2]

The work of Holmström and Milgrom implies that the potential for dysfunction arises when *any* critical dimension of effort expenditure is not measured. The words of measurement experts and practitioners reveal varying degrees of understanding of the importance of measuring all critical dimensions of effort expenditure. Most experts (see, for example, Chew, 1988; Eccles, 1991; Kaplan and Norton, 1992) recommend carefully choosing multiple measures that each represent different areas of performance. Some also recommend that chosen measures should be "balanced" (Kaplan and Norton, 1992), that they should not over-

---

[2] Not all effort dimensions are critical. Imagine a designer of can openers who expends *no* effort toward making can openers stylish. Although customers may value stylishness in a can opener, a designer devoting no effort to making a can opener stylish does not eliminate its value—an unstylish can opener still opens cans and might still be marketable.

weight one aspect of performance in comparison with others. But most do not mention the importance, implied by the H-M model, of measuring without missing any critical dimension of performance.

Experts often suggest criteria for choosing areas to measure. Robert Lewis (1955) reports use of a single question at General Electric in the early Fifties as a test of whether performance in a particular area is key:

> Will continued failure in this area prevent the attainment of management's responsibility for advancing General Electric as a leader in a strong, competitive economy, even though results in all key areas are good? (reprinted in Mason and Swanson, p. 214)

A "yes" answer to the question meant that the area was key. Clearly, key areas represent critical dimensions of effort allocation according to the earlier stated definition. But deciding on key performance measures using the General Electric test does not, by itself, rule out dysfunction. Ruling out dysfunction requires that *all* key areas are identified. The system of measurement constructed by General Electric, then, could not be considered complete without a second question being answered in the affirmative, namely, "Have all key areas been identified?" The advice of many experts is incomplete in that it provides a means of recognizing key areas but fails to address the importance of not missing key areas. This shortcoming is serious because, as Holmström and Milgrom point out, measuring only easy-to-identify or easy-to-measure areas is a flawed practice.[3] Nevertheless, there are many recognized measurement experts who expressly recommend practices that seem destined to lead to dysfunction. For example, Robert Grady and Deborah Caswell (1987) suggest a

---

[3] The flaw would disappear if there were a reason to believe that difficult-to-measure dimensions are rarely critical. But there is no obvious reason to suspect a general correspondence between ease of measurement and criticalness. In fact, many critical effort dimensions (for example, quality-related dimensions) have been observed to be especially difficult to measure (Ishikawa, 1985).

process that first identifies key areas and then pares down the set by ruling out areas that are difficult or expensive to measure. An implication of the H-M model is that Grady and Caswell's advice might be misguided.

Chapter Five:

Constructing a Model of Measurement and Dysfunction

To move analysis of incentives beyond the H-M model described in Chapter Four, it will be necessary to build a new model, the model used in the rest of this book. Before we begin, however, there are a few things that should be made clear about any modeling exercise.

What is a model? A model is a simplification; it is, by definition, a departure from reality. When reality is too complex to reason confidently about, it is often useful to extract details of a situation in the form of some simple assumptions, and then to see what can be concluded with confidence from this simpler view of the world. A model takes assumptions and converts them into corresponding conclusions. A modeling exercise is valuable, in part, because it structures reasoning and forces caution as we draw connections between assumptions and conclusions.

There are several temptations to be avoided when considering a model. One is to think that the slightest departure from a model assumption in a real situation negates the entire body of model conclusions. It is more appropriate to ask how sensitive a conclusion is to variation in a certain assumption. Often, assumptions have to be turned drastically on their heads to completely negate a model's conclusions. And such dramatic turns are often much harder to believe in than the assumption that seemed so worrying at first. In examining models, then, one should maintain a healthy skepticism about assumptions but avoid throwing the baby out with the bath water.

Another temptation to avoid is making too literal an interpretation of a model or its components. Many models contain quantities that are intangible and cannot be measured in any definitive way. The model discussed later in this book is based on assumptions about people's preferences for expending or conserving effort. Neither the preferences nor the effort are likely to be measurable in a real situation. But the model can still be useful. It is possible to agree or disagree with assumed relationships between such unmeasurable quantities (for example, do you agree or disagree that an employer's satisfaction with a worker increases as the worker chooses to work harder?). Believable relationships between unmeasurable quantities can be transformed into conclusions about behaviors that can be observed and quantities that can be measured. So don't let the fact that there is no such thing as an "effort meter" put you off of a model that makes assumptions about worker effort.

Perhaps the most common temptation people give in to when they encounter a model is to dismiss the model as being too simple to be a valid representation of real life. The model used in this book *is* simple. It is very simple at first and it becomes slightly less simple as we add factors that seem important. It is easy to complain that the model is too simple and that therefore it is not relevant to your particular situation. But it is less easy to say where in the transition from simple to complex the crucial differences arise. The special strength of modeling is in identifying these crucial differences. Models allow us to move from simple to complex in a structured way and thereby to see which added assumptions make little or no difference, and which ones turn day into night, or function into dysfunction.

The final test of the value of a model is whether it is useful or interesting to the person using it. Some valuable models are useful in a pragmatic, bottom-line sense—you can use their results to your immediate benefit. Others are useful or interesting in a broader sense, for the assistance they provide a reader who is striving to think about things in a new way. The R-H and H-M models summarized in the previous chapter succeed in the latter sense, in my view, despite the complaints I have lodged against them. They are provocative and also imperfect. I believe it is always more valuable to discuss the strengths and weaknesses of models than to attempt to rule them either valid or invalid, or realistic or unrealistic. It is in this spirit that I hope you will consider the model constructed in this book.

The Importance of the Customer

In the R-H and H-M models there were only two roles, principal and agent. The principal can be thought of as an employer and the agent as an employee. The model to be constructed here adds a third role, that of the *customer*. The customer is the purchaser of the product or service generated by the principal and agent. As in real life, the customer acts as the final judge of the value of agent effort allocations.

The three roles can be readily discerned in the examples of dysfunction presented earlier. In Blau's example, the managers of the employment agency jointly represent the principal, the employees are agents, and both the people seeking work and the firms seeking workers are customers. In the A-12 example, the program managers collectively are the principal, development team members collectively are the agent, and taxpayers and their U.S. Department of Defense representatives are the customers. In the food standards example, the Department of Agriculture is the principal, farmers are the agents, and consumers of fruits and vegetables are the customers.

The introduction of a customer who is distinct from the principal marks a point of significant departure from more traditional models (such as the R-H model). In traditional models, it is the principal's tastes that assign value to outcomes. The principal can measure the agent's true output since it is she who finally judges it. In fact, in the traditional case, the principal and the customer *are one and the same*. By not separating principal and customer, traditional models skirt questions of whether measures available to the principal represent true value.

In contrast, by separating principal and customer, the current model forces questions about the relationship between value to the customer and the measures available to the principal. The principal depends on value being produced to keep her customers happy, but she cannot directly determine the value of the agent's production—that right is reserved for the customer. The agent's payment schedule cannot, therefore, be constructed to depend on the value produced. The principal must measure proxies for value, and payment schedules must depend on the proxies instead of true output measures. Traditional presumption of easy availability of output measures must be justified. Questions of most relevance to the measurement problem become those about the imperfect nature of measures that are available to the principal. Dysfunction becomes a more worrisome possibility because imperfect measures can be subverted. The mix problem comes to the forefront.

What the Customer Wants

What does the customer want from the principal-agent team that together comprises a business firm? The customer is the beneficiary of agent effort allocations and so has preferences over agent effort allocations. For example, an employment agency customer may have opinions about how he would like the agent to divide effort between interviewing and performing referral activities. These opinions can be discussed by comparing the *customer value* of effort allocations.

For the purpose of illustration, suppose that the Blau employment agent's job consists of only two activities, both of them critical in the sense defined earlier (that is, no valuable output can be produced without devoting at least some effort to a critical activity).[1] Call the two activities *interview* and *referral*. Agent effort allocations might then be represented by a pair of effort numbers, say (5, 4), which means five units of effort devoted to interviewing and four units devoted to referral. The customer attaches value to a pair of effort numbers according to his preferences. For example, the effort allocation (5, 4) may be of more value to the customer than the allocation (3, 2). It makes sense to ask, then,

---

[1] The real employment agent's job is composed of more than two activities, of course, as are most real jobs. In terms of the modeling exercise, an extension to jobs of more than two activities is straightforward and changes none of the conclusions. Such an extension would complicate explanations and (especially) graphs, however, so I focus on the simple two-activity case in this book.

how customer preferences exhibit themselves in the rule that assigns relative values to effort allocations. For example, does an effort allocation (x, y) always have higher value than (x, y-1)? What about (x, y) versus (x-1, y+1)?

Two likely characteristics of customer preferences seem self-evident. First, it is likely that the customer would want to have effort added to an activity as long as the effort to the other activity is maintained; call this the "more is better" characteristic.[2] The customer in the Blau case would like to see extra interviews, as long as the same level of referral activity is maintained. In terms of effort numbers, (5, 4) is preferred by the customer to both (5, 3) and (4, 4).

Second, because both activities are critical, no effort to either activity means no value is produced; call this the "zero effort is awful" characteristic.[3] If all referral ceases, then nothing of value can come from the employment agency no matter how many interviews are performed. In other words, allocations of (x, 0) and (0, y) are the least preferred of all allocations, regardless of the value of x and y.

The described characteristics of customer preferences are graphed in Fig. 5.1. Think of Fig. 5.1 as a contour map of mountainous terrain; the curved lines are like lines that mark the same altitude on the contour map. The curved lines in this figure represent effort allocations that have the same value to the customer. Values corresponding to the same-value lines increase, like altitude as you move up a hill, as allocations move in the direction of the arrow. Take the allocation (3, 3): The "more is better" characteristic is apparent because allocations above and to the right of

---

[2] This is an assumption, but not a very controversial one for most situations. Still, it is important to ask whether this assumption applies in your situation.

[3] This is also an assumption about the nature of customer value. In some situations, it may not hold for all effort dimensions. In the employment office situation, it seems to hold obviously.

(3, 3) are on higher same-value lines and are thus preferred to (3, 3). The "zero effort is awful" characteristic is visible in the fact that same-value lines never intersect the axes and become bunched together closer to the axes; as allocations approach either axis, value to the customer falls off rapidly.

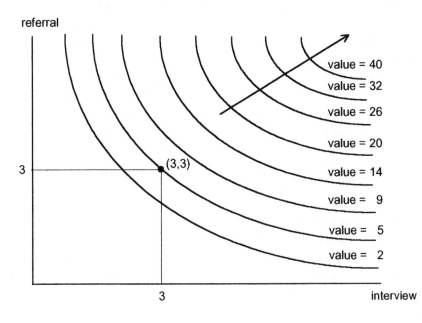

referral

value = 40
value = 32
value = 26
value = 20
value = 14
value = 9
value = 5
value = 2

3

(3,3)

3

interview

Figure 5.1: The shape of customer preferences.

Extra Effort versus Incentive Distortion

The simple representation of customer preferences (shown in Fig. 5.1) suffices to develop an intuitively appealing definition of *distortion* in a system of incentives. We are headed for discussion of an important feature of many incentive situations: *Frequently, more effort can be extracted from agents only at the price of some incentive distortion.* Whether the increase in value to the customer caused by the agent's increased effort outweighs the loss of customer value due to incentive distortion is central to motivational measurement issues. Dysfunction will later be defined with respect to exactly this trade-off. Your intuitive notions of what I mean by distortion and how it leads to dysfunction are probably roughly correct. What we need to do now, though, is make your intuition exact.

To get to a definition of incentive distortion, you must ask, How would the customer like to see the agent allocate effort? In other words, what is the customer's most preferred effort allocation? Assuming that the principal is happy when the customer is happy (because she sells more products or services and makes more revenue when the customer is satisfied), this is the same question as, How would the principal like to see agent effort allocated so long as costs of inducing the effort allocation are not a factor? The intuitive answer is that the customer and the principal would like to see the agent expend all of the effort he has and divide it between the two activities (interview and referral) in a way that maximizes customer value. The greatest amount of effort that the agent can exert is referred to here as the agent's *effort capacity*.

The effort allocation most preferred by the customer is shown in Fig. 5.2. The diagonal line represents the agent's effort capacity.[4] The highest same-value line can be reached at the point where the same-value lines and the effort capacity line are just tangent (marked A in the figure). Moving in either direction along the effort capacity line or moving underneath the line moves the allocation to a lower same-value line. Moving above the effort capacity line requires greater effort capacity.

---

[4] You may wish to verify for yourself that lines of constant effort cut across the axes at 45 degree angles. For example, one line of constant effort connects allocations (0, 4), (1, 3), (2, 2), (3, 1), and (4, 0).

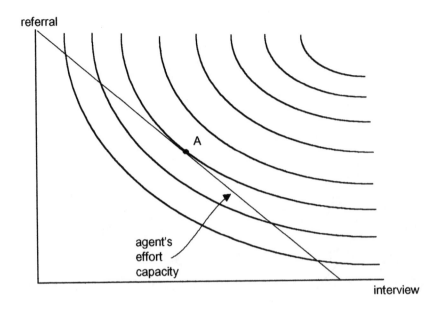

Figure 5.2: The customer's most preferred allocation.

Consider what would happen if the agent's effort capacity increased. The agent's effort capacity line would move away from the origin, making more allocations accessible. At each new level of effort capacity, there would be a new point at which the same-value lines are just tangent to the effort capacity line—a new, most preferred allocation. Allowing the effort capacity to vary from zero up to a high number causes the most preferred points to trace out a path, called the *best-mix path*. The best-mix path describes the set of allocations that maximizes value to the customer at each level of total effort expended.[5] Two examples of best-mix paths are shown in Fig. 5.3.

---

[5] In practice, it would be difficult if not impossible to actually determine a best-mix path for a real situation. That is not the purpose of this model. Even though effort and preferences are not measurable quantities, we will succeed in creating an exact notion of incentive distortion, which can be discussed. Eventually, we will use this notion to derive insights and draw conclusions about observable, measurable behavior.

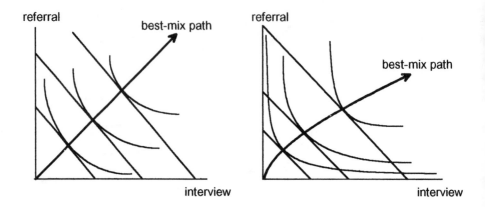

Figure 5.3: Examples of best-mix path.

The best-mix path concept is important because it provides a reference useful in evaluating incentive systems and in defining incentive distortion. One goal of incentive systems is to get more useful effort from the agent. If a system succeeds in drawing more effort out of an agent, it would also ideally cause him to divide total effort between activities in a way that keeps effort allocations on the best-mix path. An agent who is allocating effort off the path can, without expending more effort, increase value to the customer by adjusting the division of effort between activities—by moving toward the best-mix path. An incentive system that draws agent effort allocations off the best-mix path is said to be *distorted*. Distortion, then, is the property of an incentive system that causes the agent's effort allocation to leave the best-mix path, thereby seeking a less than ideal effort mix. The value of an effort allocation induced by distorted incentives is always less than the value of the undistorted allocation at the same level of total effort. It does not follow, however, that a distorted system of incentives always causes more harm than good. A system may extract more effort from an agent and simultaneously introduce distortion. If the value of extra effort extracted from the agent more than makes up for the loss in value due to distortion, then the overall outcome is favorable for the customer. Many incentive systems induce extra effort from agents at the expense of some distortion. Thus, The Crucial Test of a Motivational Measurement System:

> Does the value to the customer of the extra effort induced by a motivational measurement system more than outweigh the detrimental effects of the incentive distortion it causes?

To see how agent efforts begin to diverge from customer preferences, let us review how the agent is motivated.

Chapter Six:

Bringing Internal Motivation into the Model

The agent is motivated in three distinct ways, two of which were already discussed. As in the R-H model, the agent is eager for money and dislikes work. As before, the agent can be convinced to work harder if he is paid more, and the amount that he must be paid increases with the total level of effort. Unlike in the earlier model, however, now targets may be associated with a specific effort allocation—such as (5, 3)—rather than a total effort level—like eight total units of effort. The reason for the difference should be clear: Although the agent has equal aversion to effort expenditures required by allocations (5, 3) and (8, 0)—equal because both allocations require $5 + 3 = 8 + 0 = 8$ units of total effort expenditure—the principal prefers (5, 3) to (8, 0) because the customer does. So, if the principal can observe effort allocations on both interview and referral dimensions, she will construct a forcing contract of the form, "If you achieve the effort allocation (X, Y), I will pay you \$Z; otherwise, I will pay you nothing." As before, \$Z can be set just high enough to satisfy the agent's minimum requirements at the total effort level X+Y. And, as before, the agent will exactly meet such a contract because he gets no extra money for exceeding it but does accrue some disutility for any amount of effort he expends over the required amount. Again, as before, the principal can compare costs and benefits of achieving the possible effort allocations—

now two-dimensional—and decide on the one that maximizes her profits.

There is a very important caveat concerning the feasibility of forcing contracts: Some effort dimensions may not be observed at all. In the Blau example, interviews were counted but referral activities were not measured. In situations like this, forcing contracts can only credibly specify targets for observed dimensions. For example, the principal in the Blau case cannot say, "Do Y amount of referral activity or you will be fired," because she has no mechanism in place for verifying whether the agent has complied. Demands of this sort can be ignored by the agent with impunity. As has been noted, dimensions are frequently not observed because they are not easily observable (that is to say, observing them is impossible or prohibitively costly).

Suppose, as in Blau, that interview effort is observed but referral effort is not. In a situation like this, the principal cannot use a forcing contract to compel an agent to allocate effort on the best-mix path. She can force the agent to allocate a certain level of effort to the observed interview dimension, but the agent retains the freedom to choose referral effort as he pleases. In graphical terms, the principal can choose the horizontal coordinate of the agent's effort allocation, but the agent retains the ability to secretly choose the vertical coordinate. This gives rise to the potential for distortion of incentives.

Now consider a new element of agent motivation. Suppose that the agent gains utility from satisfying the customer (he is internally motivated). This motivation is a refinement of the Holmström and Milgrom assumption that some effort that the agent wants to expend is useful to the principal. Here, the agent knows the customer's preferences (for example, the shape of the customer's same-value lines, best-mix path, and so on) and wants to abide by them. The agent remains subject to his fondness for money and distaste for work, so there are elements of his motivation that might draw him away from best satisfying the customer. But, for all his greediness and slothfulness, the agent wants to make the customer happy.

This new element of agent motivation is important because it gives the agent reason to prefer a specific value-producing effort allocation in the absence of performance-based payments from the principal. As in the H-M model, the agent who is paid a fixed fee that does not depend on his performance will do valuable work. The difference from the H-M model is that, here, one can determine exactly which effort allocation the agent will pick when his pay does not depend on measured performance—that is, when there is no incentive system in place. Specific determination of the agent's effort allocation under *no* incentive system allows comparison with allocations that can be realized under an incentive system. As will be shown, the analysis becomes interesting when the incentive system produces a significant amount of distortion.

The Observability of Effort

Before continuing exploration of this two-dimensional model, we should address a point of potential concern. Recall that two details important to economists—namely, the unobservability of effort and the probabilistic nature of the relationship between effort and revenues—was omitted from the cost-benefit model in Chapter Four. The same details have been omitted again in the model now being developed. Here, effort can be observed directly and exactly for a specific task if it can be observed at all. This aspect of our new model demands more explanation.

In the R-H model and others like it, measurable outcomes such as revenues are sensitive to the actions of the individual agent. If the agent increases his effort, the distribution of outcomes shifts in a favorable direction. This is not an accurate picture of the situation facing most individuals in organizational settings. The actions of a lone worker within an organizational hierarchy rarely have discernible effects on overall revenues or any other firm-level measures, unless the worker is a top executive with substantial influence. It is more reasonable to assume in most organizational contexts that broad measures of organizational performance such as revenues are only nominally affected by individual agent actions. It is, rather, the sum of actions of all agents that noticeably affects revenues. So, organizations that rely solely on macro-level measures such as revenues are vulnerable to exploitation by individuals in the hierarchy who know that an individual performance will be lost in the crowd of individual performances of everyone in the hierarchy. Such agents can conserve their effort without unduly affecting what happens and without getting caught. But, of course, if everyone acts in this way, the organization's performance will be adversely impacted.

Because organizations are aware of this problem, they institute micro-level performance indicators. Micro systems take measurements at interim points in the production process that are closer to the individual. One of the desired attributes of these process measures is freedom from the probabilistic noise that complicates discernment of performance and gives risk-averse agents a reason to demand more compensation. But the measures, being interim measures, are necessarily distant from the end result—the product or service being rendered to the customer—so they are almost always imperfect proxies, far from comprehensive, and vulnerable to corruption. In such cases, risk borne by the agent ceases to be a major concern but the mix problem is very troublesome. The main problem for most incentive systems in use in real organizations is not noise in measures of performance but, rather, bias intentionally introduced by those being measured.

Model Assumptions

It has been assumed that the agent wants to provide value to the customer and knows what the customer wants. In some situations, these may be unwarranted assumptions. It is often argued that software developers have different criteria for the value of their product than do their customers. For example, programmers might value elegant code and customers might value functionality. In terms of the model developed here, this means that the customer satisfaction component of the agent's utility is not perfectly aligned with customer value. Such a situation will arise whenever the agent holds different beliefs about what constitutes value or mistaken beliefs about what the customer wants.

Another possibility is that the agent may be uncertain about what the customer wants. If the agent is risk-averse, uncertainty about what the customer wants has the effect of reducing the utility the agent gets from satisfying the customer. The result would be reduced incentive to satisfy the customer. There is evidence that this sort of problem does arise in real organizations. For example, software developers frequently demand very specific instructions and are discomfited by uncertainty about what the customer wants.

Even if the agent does have a different notion of value than the principal, however, he is still likely to provide considerable value to the customer. The best-mix path of an agent may not be identical to the best-mix path desired by the customer, but it certainly originates from the same point and has everywhere positive slope. Furthermore, the principal can abate different, mistaken, or uncertain ideas about what the customer wants by clearly communicating direction.

Effort has been assumed to be equally dear to the agent across all effort dimensions. But it is not difficult to imagine that agents may sometimes weight effort expenditure differently across dimensions. This might occur in situations in which one or more job activities are particularly dreaded by employees; for example, bank employees might avoid meetings with customers who are in difficult financial straits, or doctors might put off meetings with the family of a terminally ill patient. Unless such biases are severe, however, the value provided to the customer is still likely to be quite significant and resulting incentive distortion would be mild.

An interesting and potentially controversial aspect of the model is that the shape of customer preferences is assumed to be known by principal and agent. In real circumstances, it is unlikely that even the customer knows his preferences fully. The model therefore requires that principal and agent know the customer's preferences better than the customer does—but then so does the successful conduct of business. Before the Ford Motor Company introduced its aerostyling on the 1986 Taurus, for example, no customer would ever have identified "aerostyling-ness" as a dimension to which he would like to see agents allocate effort. Nevertheless, the customer did value aerostyling when it appeared, as was demonstrated by the booming sales of the Taurus. Ford knew better than the customer what the customer wanted—and profited handsomely from its shrewdness.

One of the tenets of product design methods like Quality Function Deployment (QFD) is that customers verbalize only the most direct of three categories of desires when asked (see, for example, Hauser and Clausing, 1988). Customers do not mention needs that they assume will be met by all products of the type in question. And they do not mention product qualities that they have not thought of but would like. They mention only qualities that they do not expect but know that they want. The model in this book assumes that the principal and agent have access to the customer's preferences across all three categories.

Chapter Seven:
Three Ways of Supervising the Agent

C onstruction of the model is now complete. What remains is to vary features of the model, to see what can be observed or concluded about an organization from this simplified picture. Of immediate interest is the observation that there are three distinct ways of managing the agent's activities available to the principal: no supervision, full supervision, and partial supervision.

No Supervision

One way the principal can manage the agent is to leave him alone. The principal measures nothing and observes no dimensions of effort allocation. Payment to the agent cannot be made contingent on performance because performance is not observed. The agent is left to work on his own and is paid a flat rate sufficient to keep him from working elsewhere. That is, the agent is *unsupervised*. This arrangement is common in some organizational settings, especially if the work being done is very specialized. The agent will do useful work in such a situation due to internal motivation alone.

The agent's *unsupervised effort allocation* provides a reference against which an incentive system can be compared. It is always of interest to ask whether the effort allocation induced by an incentive system provides more value to the customer than the unsupervised allocation. A useful incentive system should produce better results than no incentive system, because building an incentive system costs more than not building one. An incentive system should be abandoned if it provides the customer with less value than no incentive system.

Thus, the unsupervised allocation furnishes an intuitive means of defining dysfunction. *A system of incentives is dysfunctional if the resulting effort allocation provides less value to the customer than the unsupervised allocation, which arises when there is no incentive system.* Incentives may induce lower value to the customer than doing nothing if the incentives are very distorted—that is, if they draw effort allocations too far off the best-mix path. Determining how much distortion is too much requires a close examination of the unsupervised agent's behavior.

How would an unsupervised agent react? When the payment is not contingent on performance, then the agent is trading off his desire to satisfy the customer against his aversion to total effort. Figure 7.1 shows how this trade-off might unfold. Suppose an agent who is at rest allocates some effort just off the effort origin (point 1). He experiences disutility due to effort expenditure that he did not experience before (because he was expending no effort before). He also experiences new utility from making the customer more satisfied. If the utility gained from satisfying the customer in moving to point 1 is greater than the disutility due to effort, the move was a good one. The agent at point 1 notices immediately, however, that he can gain more net utility without exerting any more effort just by adjusting the division of his effort between the two effort dimensions. So, he moves along the line of constant effort until he finds a point at which the customer is most satisfied and is, therefore, most gratified in choices at this level of effort—point 2. At this point, he notices that increasing his total effort expenditure and moving a slight distance along the best-mix path, to point 3, will cause his utility from satisfying the customer to increase more than his disutility due to effort aversion. The move to point 3 will garner him more utility, so he does it. He continues in this manner, finally stopping when the next move along the best-mix path would achieve more disutility due to effort than utility due to satisfying the customer—at point 5, also labeled B. In real situations, the agent's movement to his favorite effort allocation might not evolve in exactly this way; he might move to B by way of a different path. However he arrives there, though, B is his unsupervised effort allocation.

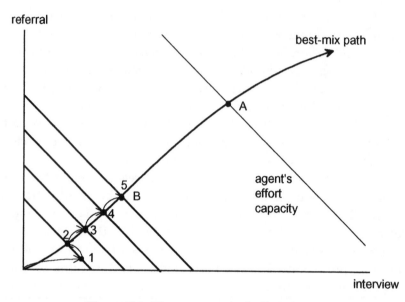

Figure 7.1: The unsupervised allocation.

The unsupervised effort allocation is good but not ideal from the viewpoint of the customer. It is good because the agent does some valuable work. It is good also because the division of effort between the two dimensions is the best possible for the given effort level; in other words, the unsupervised allocation is located on the best-mix path and is, therefore, not at all distorted. The unsupervised allocation is less than ideal, however, because it is usually well short of the allocation most preferred by the customer (point A), as was determined in Fig. 5.2. The agent is working, and doing good work, but the customer and the principal want him to work harder.

Full Supervision

Consider a situation in which the principal can measure every critical dimension of performance. Suppose, for example, that the managers of an employment office can observe both interview and referral effort expended by the agent. The agent is then *fully supervised*. Payment can be made contingent on targeted effort levels on both dimensions. The forcing contract used by the principal says to the agent, "Unless you allocate effort exactly as I specify, your minimum payment requirements will not be met." How might such a fully supervised agent react?

This is familiar territory. As long as the targeted levels are farther from the origin than the agent would otherwise be inclined to go (for example, if they are well beyond unsupervised effort levels), then the agent will meet the target exactly. Meeting the target is the only way to get paid, and allocating more effort than requested causes the agent more additional pain than pleasure (because the target is beyond the point B where the additional increments of pain and pleasure are balanced). The principal can set targets at point A, inducing the agent to expend all his effort.

The agent's fully supervised allocation is unlike the unsupervised allocation in that it is not a unique point. Rather, it occurs wherever the principal sets the target, so long as the target is located beyond the point at which the agent is inclined to allocate effort without incentives. Where the principal chooses to set targets depends on her costs (this will be discussed later). But regardless of where the fully supervised allocation is, full supervision can be a very good allocation from the viewpoints of the customer and the principal. When supervision is full, dysfunction can be prevented because effort levels can be forced on every critical dimension. The maximum value to the customer can conceivably be produced, if the principal sets targets at point A. If effort allocation is being gradually increased (as it might be if the agent's effort capacity were not exactly known to the principal), the increases can be forced to follow the best-mix path, and distortion can be avoided.

If full supervision could always be easily (that is, cheaply) achieved, it would have considerable attractions as a way to set up a measurement system. The challenge in design of a measurement system would be in finding and measuring all critical dimensions. This conception is simple, very appealing, and surprisingly common among measurement practitioners. It is natural to think of measurement in the abstract, where everything that matters can be easily measured and full supervision always is realized. Most analogies between organizational and mechanical control systems are based on such ideal abstractions. When everything that matters can be measured easily, worries about dysfunction become minor concerns about the correctness of the system's implementation. But to suppose that implementors of dysfunctional measurement systems have simply forgotten to measure one or more critical effort dimension is to ignore the measurability issue raised earlier. Many critical dimensions are not observed because they are not observable. Measures on such unobservable dimensions are either infeasible or prohibitively expensive. I will argue, in a moment, that the situation in which everything that matters can be measured easily is very rare, if it ever occurs.

Partial Supervision

No supervision and full supervision are at opposite ends of a spectrum. In the unsupervised case, no effort dimensions are measured; in full supervision, all critical dimensions are measured. What about the in-between case in which some, but not all, of the critical dimensions are measured? *Partial supervision* is by far the most interesting and realistic case. It is most interesting because it provides a basis for eventually explaining dysfunction. It is most realistic because there are almost always critical dimensions that are left unobserved, and because few organizations leave workers completely unsupervised.

In the Blau example, in which interview effort was observed but referral effort was not, payment schedules can be made contingent on interview effort alone. As long as the level of interview effort targeted by the principal is beyond what the agent is willing to expend unsupervised, the agent will meet the interviewing effort target exactly. But the agent is free to choose his effort level for referral in private, without the knowledge of the principal. How will the partially supervised agent react?

Figure 7.2 shows one way the principal-agent interaction might unfold. As in the fully supervised case, the partially supervised allocation is not a unique point. It depends, rather, on the principal's placement of a target for interviewing effort. The principal's target for interview effort draws the agent farther in the horizontal direction than he would choose to go unsupervised (point B is the unsupervised allocation). But, in moving to the higher interview-effort level, the agent realizes that he is free to choose his location on the vertical axis without danger of detection. A direct horizontal move would advance the agent to a higher level of total effort (the diagonal lines in the figure), increasing effort aversion without raising the utility for satisfying the customer by enough to compensate. By moving downward, however, the agent can move to lines of lower total effort and still meet the principal's horizontal target. Utility due to customer satisfaction is also lowered by moving downward, but at a slower rate than disutility due to effort. The point on the vertical line at which utility loss due to decrease in value is just matched by the decrease in effort disutility is the partially supervised effort allocation. The partially supervised allocation (shown as point C in Fig. 7.2) is, therefore, to the right and below the unsupervised allocation. It is not on the best-mix path, so there is some distortion. A crucial question, of course, is whether induced distortion overwhelms the favorable effect of increased effort devoted to interviewing. If so, then the incentive system is dysfunctional; if not, the incentive system constitutes constructive use of measurement under partial supervision.

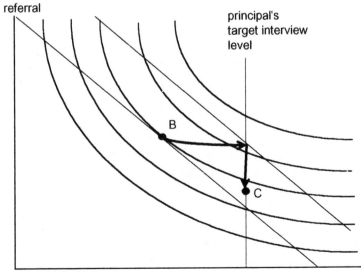

Figure 7.2: Partially supervised allocation.

Whether a partial supervision incentive system is dysfunctional depends on where the targets on observed dimensions are set. In the Blau case, imagine gradually increasing targets in the horizontal (interview) direction starting from the unsupervised allocation (point B). At each target level, the agent chooses a new vertical (referral) effort level secretly. The allocations trace out a curve, labeled *choice path* in Fig. 7.3. The choice path shows the vertical allocation that maximizes utility to the agent for each target level on the horizontal axis. The choice path turns down and to the right with increasing curvature, until it intersects and then follows the horizontal axis.

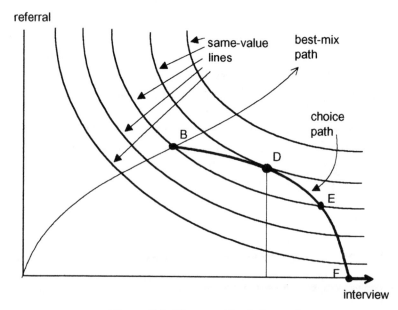

Figure 7.3: The agent's choice path.

Figure 7.3 is worth examining more closely. Following the choice path outward from the unsupervised allocation (point B), notice that value to the customer improves at first. As the target for interviewing is moved outward, the agent at first allocates effort on higher and higher same-value lines—the incentive system works. At point D, the choice path and same-value lines become tangent—the incentive system can do no better under partial supervision than when it induces an allocation at point D. There is no reason to extend targets beyond the vertical line at D because value to the customer begins to decrease along the choice path beyond that level of horizontal effort. At point E, the choice path crosses the curved same-value line that also passes through the unsupervised effort allocation. Moving targets beyond point E, then, induces dysfunction—the incentive system does harm.

Without regard to any costs of setting up targets, the principal should set the interviewing target even with the vertical line through point D under partial supervision. At this point, the agent's effort allocation is functional. But this effort allocation is not as good as the best fully supervised allocation. Some distortion is always induced by the incentive system under partial supervision; in contrast, full supervision permitted prevention of distortion. Also, under partial supervision, value to the customer increases more slowly as total effort increases than under full supervision, which allows movement along the best-mix path. If an agent wants to reach a particular level of value to the customer, he must expend more total effort along the choice path than along the best-mix path (if the level of value is even attainable along the choice path). Consequently, more aversion to effort will have to be overcome in the partially supervised case.

Chapter Eight:

Designing
Incentive Systems

The discussion thus far has focused on the agent. Now we turn to the principal to ask how she behaves in this two-dimensional situation. As before, the principal wants to maximize profit (defined as the difference between revenue generated by agent effort and the amount to be paid the agent). To increase revenues, she wants to increase value to the customer. Like the agent, she knows what the customer wants (the shape of his same-value lines, best-mix path, and so on) and wants to give him what he wants.[1] But she is also wary of the increasing costs as the agent expends more and more effort. As has already been described, she can compare costs and revenues that would result from each allocation of effort (X, Y) that she can induce from the agent, and then choose the best allocation. If these were the only costs the principal faced, this story would be over.

To be more faithful to reality, however, it is necessary to introduce the notion of *measurement cost*. Despite implicit assumptions of many managers and even measurement experts to the contrary, the costs of creating and maintaining measurement systems are significant enough to figure into cost-benefit analyses.[2]

---

[1] This is, of course, an assumption. Some possible problems with this assumption were dealt with in Chapter Six.

[2] As Tom DeMarco stated in his interview for this book, in real settings "measurement is enormously expensive."

In effect, measurement costs contribute to the total costs of making targets meaningful to the agent—targets can be meaningful only if the principal has a measurement system that can verify that targets have been met. Like the cost of paying the agent for effort, measurement costs are increasingly expensive as targets are set higher. But, unlike the cost of paying the agent for effort, measurement costs may vary across dimensions, whether interview or referral.

While the agent must be compensated equally for taking on additional effort disutility regardless of whether the increase was on interview or referral dimensions, measurement costs on the two dimensions are not likely to be equal. Further, measurement costs on different dimensions are likely to increase at drastically different rates. For example, the quality of a product or service is usually much harder and costlier to measure than its quantity. These differences in the costs of measurement enter into the cost-benefit analysis; the three modes of supervision introduced earlier are the result:

- *No supervision* results when the costs of measurement on all dimensions are high.

- *Full supervision* requires a special circumstance in which the measurement costs of all critical dimensions are low.

- *Partial supervision* results when a principal trying to maximize profits faces both low measurement cost dimensions and high measurement cost dimensions.

The importance of this conclusion is not obvious: The mode of supervision is not something that a profit-maximizing principal gets to choose. Rather, the mode of agent supervision is dictated by the structure of measurement costs in a given environment, which the principal has only limited ability to influence. In other words, a manager cannot simply choose to fully supervise employees and thereby rule out dysfunction. Some dimensions of effort will usually be too expensive to profitably measure.

Managers do not usually devote much time to thinking about things they cannot afford to find out. Instead, managers usually set out to obtain information that is available and then do with it what they can. What this discussion suggests, however, is that the dimensions that get little lasting management attention (like referral in the Blau example) are very important to understanding the appropriate way to provide employee incentives. When important dimensions are ignored, dysfunction can result from policies that encourage the agent to maximize on measured dimensions (like interviews in the Blau example).

A Better Model of Organizational Incentives

How should a principal who wants to use motivational measurement proceed?

1. The principal should determine all critical dimensions of performance for the production process at hand. This can be done using a criterion like that of Lewis (1955) detailed earlier, taking care to find all critical dimensions.

2. The principal should estimate the costs of measuring each critical dimension. There may be ways of researching this question, but answering it often primarily involves an honest common-sense assessment—how likely is it, for example, that it will be feasible to observe the amount of agent effort that goes into maintaining quality of the product or service?

3. The principal should pick the mode of supervision based on costs of measurement. If no critical dimensions can be measured at an acceptable cost, then the agent should be unsupervised. If every critical dimension can be easily measured, then full supervision should be used. If some dimensions can be easily measured but measuring others is exceedingly expensive, then partial supervision should be instituted.

4. The principal should set targets in a manner appropriate to the mode of supervision selected. If the agent is unsupervised, no target setting is necessary. If full supervision occurs, then agents can be encouraged to maximize on all measured dimensions; distortion can be prevented and targets can be kept on the best-mix path. Partial supervision will be effective when targets are set at a moderate level on measurable dimensions and agents are discouraged from exceeding targeted levels of performance. Under partial supervision, dysfunction will result eventually if levels of effort are permitted to increase without appropriate boundaries.

Several points about the three modes of supervision need to be emphasized. One important point is the desirability of achieving full supervision. When full supervision is achieved, dysfunction can be prevented, and agents can be encouraged to work hard in the interests of the organization. Payment schedules become simple because the agent can be encouraged to maximize on all performance measures. Measures can even be combined into a single measure of performance in a way that causes the agent to follow the best-mix path as he attempts to meet his own needs.

The advantages of full supervision—that is, of measuring comprehensively—are recognized by some measurement experts. Eccles and Pyburn, for example, title their 1992 paper "Creating a Comprehensive System to Measure Performance." Larry Putnam, in his interview for this book, asserted that

> There has to be at least a minimum degree of comprehensiveness so that people can't focus on loading the dice and making themselves look good without really accomplishing what management intends.

This statement is interesting in two ways: First, it suggests not only that comprehensiveness is a desirable characteristic in a measurement system, but also that it is an essential characteristic if dysfunction is to be prevented; further, it recognizes the importance of measuring all critical dimensions. Second, and less in keeping with the model developed in this book, this viewpoint assumes that comprehensiveness is generally achievable and desirable.

The model developed in the previous chapters suggests that it may not be profitable to achieve full supervision in every situation because of the high cost of measuring one or more critical dimensions. No matter how vehemently someone recommends comprehensive systems of measurement or how persuasively he advocates the benefits of full supervision, whether full supervision can be profitably realized depends on costs of measuring different dimensions of performance. Costs of measuring are a characteristic of the environment and the task being measured. Consequently, the profit-maximizing principal has limited ability to choose her own mode of supervision. She must, rather, react appropriately to the situation facing her. However badly she might want to use full supervision, it may not maximize profit in some circumstances. Often, it is possible to redesign jobs and tasks so that measurement costs are reduced. But there are limits on cost reductions that are beyond the control of the principal.

Measurement experts interviewed for this book differ considerably in their evaluations of the feasibility of full supervision. Jones stated that nothing is too difficult or too costly to measure if one is clever. Likewise, Expert X asked, "Can [measurements] be so robust that people can't tamper with them?—Yes." Card asserted that the system of measurement he has in place in his organization is comprehensive and constitutes proof that it can be done. In sharp contrast, McGregor (1960), Ridgway (1956), Ishikawa (1985), DeMarco, and Ed Tilford all deny that comprehensive measurements are possible at reasonable cost, at least in many environments. DeMarco offered an observation quite consistent with the analysis of the previous section:

> [It has been said that] . . . there's always some way of measuring something . . . if you need to know that thing. . . . But it matters how much you need to know it compared to what it costs. That's a fair analysis to make.

DeMarco also emphasized the inability to verify performance in most production environments, especially where knowledge workers are concerned.

Some measurement proponents argue that systems that are not comprehensive can become comprehensive at low cost, or no cost, when they are supplemented by subjective corrections to measured evaluations of performance. Eccles (1991) states the case for subjective correction in this way:

> The difficulty of aligning incentives to performance is heightened by the fact that formulas for tying the two together are rarely effective. Formulas have the advantage of looking objective, and they spare managers the unpleasantness of having to conduct truly frank performance appraisals. But if the formula is simple and focuses on a few key variables, it inevitably leaves some important measures out. Conversely, if the formula is complex and factors in all of the variables that require attention, people are likely to find it confusing and may start to play games with the numbers. Moreover, the relative importance of the variables is certain to change more often—and faster—than the whole incentive system can change (p. 135).

Having established in just a few sentences a seemingly powerful case against measurement-based control, Eccles rescues his favored management method by recourse to subjective corrections:

> For these reasons, I favor linking incentives strongly to performance but leaving managers free to determine their subordinates' rewards on the basis of all the relevant information, qualitative as well as quantitative. Then it is up to the manager to explain candidly to subordinates why they received what they did (p. 135).

Watts Humphrey and Bill Curtis (1991) similarly invoke subjective correction in response to claims that a standard method for auditing and evaluating government software contractors causes the audited organizations to try to cheat to achieve higher ratings. They argue that the on-site interview part of the evaluation method allows subjective corrections to compensate for any manipulation by contractors of the formal measurement instrument (a questionnaire).

There are reasons to believe, however, that subjective corrections are well short of costless panaceas for achieving full supervision. Pat Larkey and Jonathan Caulkins (1992) document the pathologies that arise in the course of the kind of subjective performance evaluation that Eccles advocates. Eccles stresses the importance of "truly frank performance appraisals" and candid explanations of why some employees are rewarded more than others. Larkey and Caulkins provide convincing evidence that the required frankness and candor is rarely realized in actual practice and that, in fact, managers often do not provide the required correction because it is easier to defend ratings consistent with formal indicators of performance. Tilford, based on his own experience as a manager, flatly rejected Humphrey and Curtis' assertion that subjective correction makes manipulation of software contractor audit results impossible:

> I've had [audits] done on me. . . . I saw folks come in who were doing assessments that weren't really knowledgeable about software processes, and who really had a hard time auditing the company, and I realized that if we wanted to, we could blow them away. . . .

Robyn Dawes (1988) cites extensive research that shows that people's confidence in their ability to make subjective corrections to measured evaluations far exceeds their actual ability.

Whether or not full supervision can be attained in most situations, it is probably safe to assert that partial supervision is the most commonly realized mode of supervision in real settings; most real jobs involve some aspects that are easy to measure and others that are difficult to measure. Two performance dimensions that appear in a great many real circumstances are *quantity* and *quality*. There almost always is something that can be counted at every stage in a production process. Likewise, there almost always is some issue as to the quality of the product or service, and quality is notoriously difficult to assure, especially in its more subtle aspects. As Ishikawa (1985) notes, you may succeed in achieving quality in the sense of meeting specification and still the customer may not be satisfied. Quality is, by its nature, ephemeral; it is whatever the customer says it is, regardless of how vehemently some quality experts may cling to definitions like "conformance to specification." The difficulty of verifying quality is heightened when production activity is largely mental, hence not directly observable, as in many professional settings such as software development.

Amid the difference of opinions about the feasibility of comprehensive measurement systems, an explanation of dysfunction begins to appear. The principal who believes she has achieved full supervision when she has, in fact, achieved partial supervision might set targets too far out on measured dimensions. She might encourage maximization of the agent's performance measures when measurements beyond a certain level should be discouraged. How this mistake might arise will be discussed later, but it is already easy to see how such an error might propagate dysfunction, as the agent moves effort from unmeasured to measured dimensions.

Chapter Nine:

A Summary of the Model

Much new material has been presented in the previous four chapters, and it is worthwhile now to summarize the model as it has been discussed. This model, like all models, is a simplification of reality. It can, nevertheless, structure our reasoning usefully and raise provocative issues.

The Model Setup

Chapter Five began with a job that is composed of only two activities. In the situation described by Blau, for example, employment agents perform both an interview activity and a referral activity. Most jobs are more complex than this (including, no doubt, the job described in the Blau example), but explanations are easier if we keep things simple.[1]

There are three people involved in this simplified job situation. The principal is the employer. She is the person who controls the facilities (desks, telephones, and so on, in the Blau example) needed to do the job. The agent is the employee. The principal hires the agent to use the available facilities to do the actual

---

[1] The arguments presented in this book can be extended to more complex jobs of many activities without altering the conclusions.

work involved in the job (interviewing and referral, in the Blau example). The third person in the modeled situation is the customer. The customer uses the output of the job. So it is the customer—and only the customer—who can place a value on the work that the agent does using the principal's facilities.[2]

Customers have preferences about how the agent expends effort. For example, customers of the Blau employment agency probably don't want agents to spend all their time interviewing; if they do, no one will ever be placed and nothing of value will result from the job done by the interviewer. As the customer thinks about how the agent might expend his effort, the customer can say how he would like each additional unit of effort generated by the agent to be expended. For example, if an agent offers to expend two more units of effort, the customer might say, "Expend one unit on interviewing job candidates and the other unit on calling prospective employers." If a third unit of effort becomes available, the customer might say, "Use that unit of effort on interviewing." And so on. If the agent and the customer continued in this manner, you could draw a picture of customer preferences like the one in Fig. 9.1. The roughly diagonal line in the figure shows how the customer wants agent effort to increase. This line is called the *best-mix path*, because it shows the mix of effort that is best from the customer's perspective, for every possible level of agent effort expenditure.

The principal depends for her livelihood on keeping the customer happy, so the principal wants the agent to do work just the way the customer wants it. The principal is willing to incur some costs to encourage the agent to do things the customer's way.

Chapter Six showed that there is a point, however, at which it becomes too costly to convince the agent to do work in a way that satisfies the customer. The agent also likes keeping customers happy and is inclined to expend effort in the mix that the customer desires. But the agent gets tired as he expends more and more effort. Left on his own, the agent will expend up to a cer-

---

[2] In the Blau example, the managers of the employment agency jointly represent the principal. The employees are the agents, and both the people seeking work and the firms seeking employees are customers.

tain amount of effort in the mix desired by the customer. The agent must receive extra encouragement to go beyond this certain amount. Payment by the principal is a common form of extra encouragement for the agent.

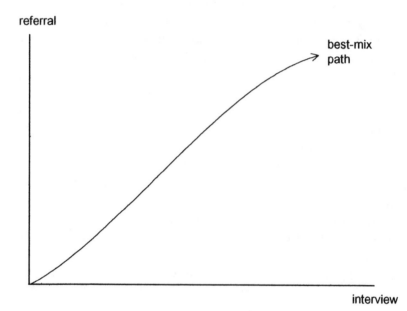

Figure 9.1: How the customer wants effort to increase.

Three Ways of Supervising the Agent

Here is the situation at the beginning of Chapter Seven: The customer has ideas about how he would like to see effort increase. The agent is willing to provide effort in the manner the customer desires—up to a point. The principal wants the customer to be as happy as possible, so she wants to find ways of getting the agent to expend more effort for the customer. An important consideration for the principal, however, is the cost of getting more effort from the agent. The principal can face three distinct cost situations.

If the principal is very lucky, she may find herself in a position in which she can measure the agent's effort expenditure in all activities at very low cost. In this situation, the principal can say things to the agent like, "If you do fifteen interviews and twenty referrals, I will give you a bonus of $X."[3] This situation is called *full supervision* and is ideal from the principal's point of view. The agent can be encouraged to work very hard in the manner desired by the customer at low cost to the principal. The customer will be happy and the principal will do well.

At the opposite end of the cost spectrum, the principal may find that measuring the agent's effort expenditure is very costly for all activities. This might happen if the job involves activities that are very intangible or if the agent has specialized expertise so that the principal is not really qualified to judge his performance. This situation is called *no supervision*. In this situation, the principal has little recourse but to leave the agent unmeasured and accept the amount of effort that the agent is willing to provide on his own. To force more effort from the agent would cost the principal too much. This situation is not ideal from the principal's point of view, because she has little control over the agent. But it is not a terrible position for the principal because the customer does get some value from the agent's work and the mix of the effort will be just as is desired by the customer.

Between these two extreme situations is one in which some, but not all, of the agent's effort expenditure can be measured at low cost. In the Blau example, suppose that interviewing can be easily measured but referral is more intangible, therefore prohibitively costly to measure. This situation is called *partial supervision*. In this case, the principal can provide bonuses to the agent but only for the activities that can be measured at acceptable cost. In the Blau example, the principal can credibly say, "If you do fifteen interviews, I will give you a bonus of $X," but she is not credible if she offers a bonus for performance on the referral

---

[3] The encouragement provided by the principal might not be so explicit. A promise of more rapid career advancement for strong output on measured dimensions is essentially equivalent to an explicit bonus for the modeled situation.

dimension. The agent knows that the principal has no way of measuring performance on the referral activity at acceptable cost, so the agent is free to choose effort expenditure with impunity.

Figure 9.2 shows what happens as the principal adds bonuses and other encouragements on the activity for which she has available measurements (interviewing). As the principal promises bonuses at higher levels of interviews, the agent performs at those levels. At first, the agent's desire to do what the customer wants weighs heavily in his choice of the mix of effort. So, at first (that is, at lower levels of interviews), the agent's effort allocation stays close to the best-mix path. As the principal provides more extreme inducements, however, the agent's desire to provide the mix of effort wanted by the customer gets overwhelmed. The agent's effort allocation moves away from the best-mix path. The gap that appears between the agent's effort allocation and the best-mix path represents *incentive distortion.* The path that shows how the effort allocations move as the encouragements become more extreme is called the *choice path,* as shown in Fig. 9.2.

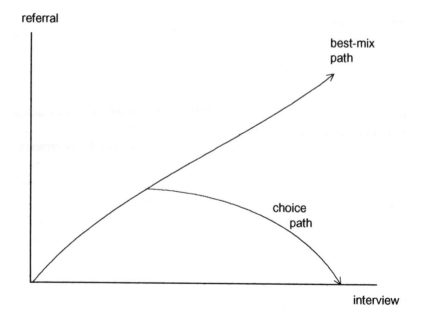

Figure 9.2: Partial supervision.

The important question, of course, is what happens to value to the customer as the agent's effort allocation follows the choice path (and as incentive distortion increases). Do the principal's bonuses do good for the customer? Or do they cause dysfunction? Chapter Seven showed in detail that, at first, the principal's encouragements on the interview activity produce more value for the customer. As inducements become more extreme and the agent reaches higher levels of interviews, however, value to the customer begins to decrease. Eventually, value to the customer will be lower than it would be if the agent were left unsupervised. An incentive system becomes *dysfunctional* when it begins to reduce value to the customer below what it would be in the case of an unsupervised agent.

An important conclusion that derives from this analysis is that a principal should manage very differently in partial supervision than she does in full supervision. In full supervision, because all activities can be measured, any increase in effort by the agent provides additional value to the customer. So, the principal should aggressively induce greater and greater levels of effort from the agent. In partial supervision, however, increases in effort beyond a certain point reduce value to the customer. In such a case the principal should set targets more moderately and perhaps even penalize overperformance in a particular activity.

Within this conclusion are the beginnings of an explanation of dysfunction in real organizations. Suppose a principal believes she faces a fully supervised situation when she actually is facing a partially supervised situation. She will aggressively encourage the agent to expend high levels of effort (as is appropriate in full supervision). The agent will comply, but only on measured activities. To achieve the high levels being targeted by the principal on measured activities, the agent will starve unmeasured activities that are also important to the value of his work. The customer will get little value as the mix of effort provided by the agent grows ever farther from the mix desired by the customer.

The Principal's Solution

Chapter Eight pointed out that the principal does not get to choose her supervisory situation. She cannot simply decide that she prefers full supervision, for example. Whether a principal faces a situation in which no, partial, or full supervision can be achieved is largely determined by the nature of the job being supervised. It is a characteristic of the organizational setting. In the long term, the principal has some ability to influence the organizational setting and the design of the job, and might thereby change the cost of measuring certain activities. In most cases, however, the principal cannot take simple actions to render less expensive what was formerly expensive. An activity that is costly to measure will remain so, no matter how vehemently a principal may want to measure everything of importance. Some things (in fact, many things) are just not easy to measure.

Chapter Ten:

Measurement and Internal Motivation

There is more to be said about motivation and measurement than was covered in Chapters Five through Nine. To go beyond measurement-based control requires broadening of the discussion in two respects: First, internal motivation must be considered as a viable means of encouraging members of an organization to achieve satisfactory effort levels; in this context, structural advantages of control methods that rely on internal motivation can be demonstrated. Second, the possibility of measurement that is intended to be purely informational must be examined; then, questions about the feasibility of purely informational measurement and about competing designs of informational measurement systems can be addressed.

Internal versus External Motivation

The difference between internal and external motivation is elusive because an expected external payback can be presumed as explanation for almost any act. When a person does a good deed in secret, it can be argued that motivation for the act came from within. But if one assumes that the do-gooder believed at the moment of action that there was a significant and foreseeable probability of detection, then the expectation of accolades might be said to be an external benefit that explains the action. Even if there was no chance that the good deed would be discovered, assumed religious or metaphysical beliefs might provide a reason to call the motivation external. A person who justifies a good deed done in secret by saying, "I believe that what goes around, comes around" is reacting to an intangible but external incentive.

Many systems in use in real organizations rely on obviously external incentives to motivate workers. A sales quota that pays a bonus to a salesperson who sells more than a certain number of computers in a month is one example of a commonly used form of external incentive. A slightly more subtle example is a system that requires commitment by a manager to a 10 percent cost reduction in his area of responsibility. There may be no certain monetary bonus associated with meeting the goal, but failing to meet it carries the expectation of diminished career prospects.

Instances of internal motivation can also be found. Casual experience suggests that there are honest salespeople who refuse to exaggerate in describing their product's features, thereby losing sales and commission payments to salespeople who are less honest. It is possible to invent an external explanation for the actions of an honest salesperson or for anyone else who chooses to "do the right thing." One might suppose, for example, that honest salespeople are prone to imagine scenarios of retribution in which dishonest people are found out and punished. But the presumption of such reveries to explain the actions of all who make seemingly unselfish choices is vacuous and unsatisfying. Whatever specific thoughts inhabit the mind of an honest salesman, what is most important is that he has abandoned formal definitions of performance in favor of his own values and discretion, often to his immediate material detriment.

External motivation might be defined as a tendency to act in response to promises of rewards for performance according to mutually known criteria that are set down in advance by the promisor. In contrast, internal motivation might be defined as a tendency to act as compelled by private expectations of performance according to the action-taker's own personal criteria. When targets are external, performance is objectively discernible. Concern with objective definitions of performance is, then, a trait of those who are externally motivated. Conversely, when motivation is internal, performance is a matter to be determined by the action-taker's personal judgment. Concern with personal, subjective codes of behavior is a characteristic of those who are internally motivated.

The decision to rely on external motivation, whether in practice or in constructing a model, implies conservative assumptions about human motivation. Among the usual assumptions is that internal motivation is not adequate to produce the performance required by the instigators of organizational activity. A widely adopted set of assumptions that leads to reliance on external incentives is often labeled rational self-interest. According to the doctrine of rational self-interest, people take no actions that do not lead to net *monetary* benefit to the action-taker. All actions are therefore selfish in a very narrow sense. Internal motivation does not exist or is irrelevant to agent action, at least in the long run. Obtaining cooperation becomes a matter of correctly arranging bonuses, payment schedules, and other contingent promises.

The rational self-interest framework is attractive to economists in part because it is simple. Models based on rational self-interest are more likely to be mathematically tractable than models based on more complex assumptions. But the validity of rational self-interest assumptions has been frequently called into question by social scientists (see, for example, Simon, 1983) and managers.

Recall that Barnard's (1938) inducements and contributions framework also requires net benefit to employees as a condition of continued involvement in the enterprise. Similar notions are common in behavioral theories of motivation within organizations (see March and Simon, 1958; Thompson, 1967; Vroom and Deci, 1970). The difference between many behavioral theories and rational self-interest models is that the former define benefit and cost more broadly. Barnard holds that "the unaided power of material incentives . . . is exceedingly limited" (p. 143). Under his and other behavioral theories, benefits can include monetary gains, feelings of fulfillment for a job well done, and gratification from sharing in an organization's success. Costs can include feelings of disappointment due to one firm's performance being overshadowed by a different firm, loss of self-esteem due to general feelings of failure, and so on.

A subfield of organizational behavior, known as the Human Relations School (HRS), has devoted itself to disputing the validity of rational self-interest models and proposing models based on less restrictive assumptions (see, for example, Roesthlisberger and Dickson, 1939; Argyris, 1952; McGregor, 1960; Likert, 1961, 1967; Ouchi, 1979, 1981). As summarized below, McGregor's widely cited definitions of Theory X and Theory Y styles of management outline the terms of the debate.

Theory X refers to the style of management that results when managers believe that people: 1) dislike work and attempt to avoid it; 2) must be coerced, controlled, directed, and threatened in order to put forth effort toward the achievement of organizational objectives; and 3) prefer to be treated this way because they are inherently unambitious and want to avoid responsibility. Not surprisingly, Theory X managers are entirely concerned with the design and implementation of external motivation schemes, which force employees to do what is required to further the goals of the organization, since there is no other means of motivating employees under this theory.

Theory Y management style arises when managers assume that people: 1) consider that expenditure of effort in work is as natural as play or rest; 2) capably exercise self-direction and self-control in the service of objectives to which they are committed; and 3) seek responsibility and exercise creativity in solving problems. Theory Y managers consider external motivation schemes only one way of motivating and are therefore concerned also with inspiring internal motivation, by example and through persuasion, and in clearly communicating direction to employees.

Theories X and Y represent poles of a continuum. Where a particular management style falls on the continuum depends on management's underlying judgment about relative strengths of external and internal motivation. Rational self-interest and Theory X models rely on implicit assumptions that external motivation is a stronger and more reliable way of motivating employees. But there is evidence that internal motivations can be very strong. Simon (1991) notes that people identify with the organizations where they work as they do with their family, or with a favorite sports team, experiencing feelings of exhilaration and dismay as the fortunes of the group rise and fall. Dawes (1991) has conducted experiments that place people in situations in which their individual interests are in conflict with the interests of a group. He finds that people are willing to sacrifice their own interests in favor of group interests when they identify even slightly with the group.[1] William Ouchi (1981) argues that "clan mechanisms" (such as feelings of group identity, desires for group membership, and so on) strongly influence behavior in successful organizations. He suggests that Japanese firms have set the world standard for quality in the manufacture of complex products because they have been successful at inspiring feelings of group identity and desires to do what is good for the company. Semco, a Brazilian company, provides an illustration of the power of internal motivation and the capacity of individuals for self-direction that is as compelling as it is unusual:

> At Semco, a Brazilian manufacturer of pumps, mixers, valves, and catering and other industrial equipment, most employees decide their own salaries. Their bonuses, which are tied to the company's profits, are shared out as they choose. Everyone, including factory workers, sets his own working hours and groups of employees set their own productivity and sales targets. There are no controls over travel or business expenses. There are no manuals or written procedures. Workers choose their own boss and then publicly evaluate his performance. All employees have unlimited access to the company's books and are trained to read balance sheets. Everyone knows what everyone else earns, and some workers earn more than their boss. Big corporate decisions, such as diversifications and acquisitions, are made by all employees . . . ("Diary of an Anarchist," *The Economist*, June 26, 1993, p. 66).

---

[1] In one experiment, groups of people who had only a few minutes of shared experience, and who were defined as groups only because their members had each drawn chips of the same color from a bag in a random drawing, began to exhibit willingness to sacrifice for the group and showed out-group feelings toward the group composed of people who had drawn different-colored chips from the bag.

Semco's methods would look reckless to most Western managers, seeming a sure example of anarchy that would lead inevitably to financial ruin.[2] And yet,

> Semco has survived, and sometimes even thrived, amid the turmoil of Brazil's hyper-inflationary economy, which has obliterated thousands of other small manufacturers. . . . Semco [is projected] to earn about $3 million on sales of some $30 million this year. . . . Today the firm is debt-free and has nearly 300 workers, with another 200 running their own "satellite" businesses, set up as independent contractors with Semco's help. . . . because a large proportion of the earnings of all employees is also tied directly to the firm's profits, peer pressure on employees not to abuse their freedoms is enormous. "It's really very simple," says [the firm owner]. "All we're really doing is treating people like adults" (*The Economist, loc. cit.*).

Rensis Likert (1961) and fellow members of the HRS have compiled an empirical literature that suggests that Theory Y methods are not only effective but have long-term advantages over Theory X methods.

As has been mentioned, external motivation models like that of Ross and Holmström rule out Theory Y modes of motivation. From this perspective, workers' "preferences are important premises of organizing, but they are not instruments of organization" (Leavitt and March, in Williamson, 1990, p. 13). Worker behavior can be affected only by adjusting the worker's surroundings. But as behavioral scientists ranging from Barnard (1938) to Barbara Leavitt and coauthor James March have noted, another way of changing worker behavior is to lead or inspire— to change not the array of carrots and sticks in the surroundings, but rather *what workers want and how they feel about the organization.* This approach emphasizes "conscious attention to the transformation of preferences" (Leavitt and March, *loc. cit.*). Such a transformation may be brought about by force of leadership per-

---

[2] For more details on Semco's unique management approach, see Semler (1993).

sonality, by appeals to patriotism or passions, by honest efforts to promote trust in the work community, by cementing the relationship between organization and worker (as in the Japanese practice of lifetime employment), or by a variety of other means. Jeffery Liker *et al.* (1993) find, in support of the last method, that Japanese companies seem to intentionally create reciprocal vulnerabilities to exploitation between themselves and their suppliers. When everyone is vulnerable to covert exploitation, it is not unusual for human beings to "pull together" and forego opportunities for exploitation, for the good of the whole. The Semco example and the Dawes experiments also lend credence to this hypothesis.

Leavitt and March summarize Barnard's position on the role of transformation of preferences in a statement representative of the views of many behavioral scientists and practitioners:

> In modern terms, Barnard proposed that an executive create and sustain a culture of beliefs and values that would support cooperation. The appeal is not to exchanges, Pareto optimality, or search for incentive schemes; it is to the construction of a moral order in which individual participants act in the name of the institution—not because it is in their self-interest to do so, but because they identify with the institution and are prepared to sacrifice some aspects of themselves for it (Leavitt and March in Williamson, 1990, p. 13).

Delegatory Management

Regardless of how internal motivation is achieved, its characteristics relative to external motivation are worth examining. The style of management that relies on internal motivation, and that contrasts sharply with measurement-based management, is here called *delegatory management*. Delegatory management changes the agent's preferences. The weighting of two components of the agent's utility is adjusted. The agent is made to feel disutility for effort less acutely, inspired by enthusiasm for the mission of the organization, or by the persuasiveness of its leader. Or, the agent is convinced to value customer satisfaction more highly than he did previously, for similar reasons. It is as if coefficients for each component of utility are being adjusted upward or downward.

The effect of changing the weighting between components of utility is to change the agent's unsupervised effort allocation. As weight is shifted away from disutility for effort toward utility for satisfying the customer, the unsupervised allocation moves outward from the origin in a way that improves value to the customer. Notice also that the unsupervised allocation always moves along the best-mix path (see Fig. 10.1). As long as the agent considers all effort expended to be equivalent (that is, as long as he does not, for example, dread interviewing more than referral activities—a possibility that was discussed in Chapter Six), and as long as agent utilities are aligned with customer value, his unsupervised allocation will be on the best-mix path. Thus, delegatory management increases value to the customer without inducing any distortion at all. This fact constitutes a potential reason to prefer delegatory management over measurement-based management. Among other things, it means that delegatory management used by itself (that is, when there is no supervision) cannot cause the sort of dysfunction that is sometimes caused by measurement-based management.

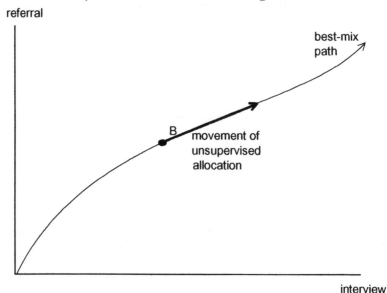

Figure 10.1: How delegatory management
affects the unsupervised effort allocation.

Of course, changes in the weighting of the agent's utility components are not achieved without cost to the principal. Taking time from production activities to promote group identity, extending lifetime employment to workers, and similar steps all involve costs to the principal. In keeping with the assumptional form of argument in earlier chapters, assume that the cost grows at an increasing rate as the agent's effort allocation is moved outward on the best-mix path. As before, there is a point at which the cost to the principal of inducing an additional increment of value from the agent is just offset by the utility of that incremental increase. This is the point at which a shrewd principal will choose to set her delegatory management; this is the amount of organizational identification that should be "purchased" by the principal. Here, devotion to the organization and its related benefits become too costly to procure.

The Conflict Between Measurement-Based and Delegatory Management

It is reasonable to ask why the principal cannot use delegatory and measurement-based management simultaneously, paying costs for each while they provide more valued returns. The principal might use delegatory management to move the unsupervised effort allocation out along the best-mix path until the marginal disutility from cost of delegation equals the marginal utility provided to the principal by increased customer value. Then, measurement-based incentives could be used to force even more effort from the agent.

However, there is reason to believe that the methods should not be used together. Empirical work on human motivation (Frey, 1993; Deci and Ryan, 1985; McGraw, 1978) has shown that external motivators often crowd out internal motivation. This means that measurement-based management is in conflict with delegatory management. There is a negative interaction because of the implicit message of distrust that a measurement system conveys by the fact of its existence. The offer of an external reward for that which would otherwise be provided because of internal motivation may also have an insulting or debasing effect that lowers internal motivation (Hirsh, 1976). DeMarco said of performance measurement:

> It's demeaning. . . . People are motivated by extrin-
> sics and intrinsics and the intrinsics are much more
> powerful—the pride and workmanship, the enjoy-
> ment of doing things with your colleagues. . . . But
> the extrinsics shove the intrinsics aside. Say you
> give me an extrinsic reason to do this. I lose track of
> whether I'm having a good time working with my
> colleagues on this goal.

All the interviewed experts referred to the tendency of those
being measured to see the act of measurement in an unfavorable
light, at least at first. Alfie Kohn (1993) observes that measurement connotes comparability which, in turn, fosters competition
and even unfriendly feeling between workers, thereby undermining any sense of common purpose. Bruno Frey (1993) identifies a
"spillover effect" that suggests that measuring worker activity
within one area has a detrimental effect on internal motivation in
other areas.[3]

In terms of the model developed in Chapters Five through
Eight, the conflict between delegation and measurement means
that the mere introduction of measurement-based controls moves
the unsupervised allocation toward the point (0, 0), opposite of
what is desired. This established empirical fact provides justification for the assumption that the principal must often choose

---

[3] The psychology literature (see Deci and Ryan, 1985, for references) treats the
nature of this interaction between internal and external motivation in much
greater detail. The negative interaction that results in "crowding out" is
attributed to a shift in locus of control from agent to principal that reduces the
agent's sense of self-determination (DeCharms, 1968; Deci, 1971), and to the
cognitive dissonance (Festinger, 1957) created when an agent who had supposed himself to be internally motivated is confronted by an external reward
that seems to imply otherwise. This literature also describes a "crowding in"
phenomenon (Frey, 1993), wherein external rewards actually increase intrinsic
motivations. The conditions necessary for this to occur, however—that
rewards and punishments seem to fairly distinguish between agents of high
and low internal motivation—seem to require that full supervision is realized.

between measurement and delegation as she manages an organization. When the interaction effect is strong, using both methods would never be preferred to using either individually (Frey, 1993). It is instructive to compare the two options as if they were exclusive and to compare the advantages of each.

Chapter Eleven:

Comparing Delegatory and Measurement-Based Management

When comparing delegatory and measurement-based management, the principal should weigh the total profits provided by the optimal investment in each individually. The optimal investment in measurement results in no supervision, full supervision, or partial supervision; the optimal investment in delegation results in a particular placement of the unsupervised effort allocation on the best-mix path. The type of supervision that results and where delegation puts the effort allocation after the optimal investment in measurement or delegation, respectively, depend on characteristics of the organization, the task being performed, and the inherent internal motivation of employees. Without specifying costs and utilities explicitly, we cannot say what mode of supervision or delegatory allocation will result, or which method of management should be preferred by the principal. However, qualitative observations about the suitability of measurement and delegation in different situations are possible.

If cost of measurement is so low on all dimensions that the agent can be forced to exert maximum effort, then measurement-based incentives can provide the outcome most highly valued by the principal. This situation permits an extreme form of full supervision, here called *best-case full supervision*, in which the principal can gainfully compel the agent to move along the best-mix path all the way to his effort capacity. Maximum value can be provided to the customer; distortion can be completely prevented. It may be possible for optimal investment in delegatory management to provide the same outcome, but this would require that it is easy to inspire agents to expend as much effort as they can. Such commitment to an organization probably occurs but is surely uncommon. Thus, measurement-based management seems recommended in this situation. (This situation is probably quite rare, however.) Where cost of measurement is so low across all of the agent's tasks, tasks must be simple and easy to observe and to understand.

If the form of full supervision that can be realized in a situation is not best-case, that is, if some measurement is recommended on every dimension but measuring out to the agent's effort capacity on every dimension is *not* recommended (due to relatively high cost on at least one dimension)—then measurement-based management gets a more limited endorsement. The principal's optimal target in these situations will not, in general, be on the best-mix path. So, there will be some incentive distortion. Since moving *off* the best-mix path to a given level of customer value is more expensive in terms of agent effort than moving *along* the path, value is procured by the principal at a higher cost here than under best-case full supervision. Consequently, the level of profit to the principal is lower than when best-case supervision can be achieved. As value to the customer grows more expensive, delegation gains relative appeal. It is possible that agents are so poorly motivated to start with or that extra effort induced from the agent using delegatory management is costly enough that optimal investment in delegation yields less overall utility to the principal. But if the cost of delegation is relatively low and therefore optimal investment in delegation results in relatively high value to the customer, delegation may be recommended.

Under partial supervision, getting to a particular customer value level is more costly in terms of agent effort than if movement of the allocation were along the best-mix path. Since at least one critical dimension is not measured, allocations induced by partial supervision are farther off the best-mix path (that is, they involve even more distortion) than in full supervision that is not best-case. So, in most cases, partial supervision yields still lower profits for the principal, compared to even full supervision that is not best-case. Furthermore, partial supervision, unlike full supervision, permits dysfunction. In full supervision of any type, dysfunction can be avoided because measurement is done on every critical dimension. In partial supervision, at least one critical dimension is not measured. Targets set badly on the measured dimensions can, therefore, cause dysfunction. Overall, delegation compares favorably to partial supervision because delegation cannot cause dysfunction, or even distortion, and the movement along the best-mix path that it causes is more efficient in producing value for each unit of agent effort expended.

Situations that call for no supervision, although they are more common than is usually conceded, do not offer very interesting comparisons between measurement-based and delegatory management. If costs are high on all dimensions, then a no supervision situation results from optimal investment in measurement. The principal is better off letting the agent work on his own. Delegatory management is, then, the only means available for increasing value to the customer. Table 11.1 summarizes the management recommendation as delegation costs and the supervisory situations that result from the structure of measurement costs vary.

Table 11.1.
Recommended Management Methods.

	No Supervision	Partial Supervision	Full Supervision	Best-Case Full Supervision
Low Delegation Costs	Delegation	Delegation	Delegation or Measurement	Measurement
High Delegation Costs	Nothing Works	Measurement with Precautions Against Dysfunction	Measurement	Measurement

The cell in Table 11.1 that is applicable to a particular situation can be determined by examining the characteristics of the situation. Doing this requires some idea of the organizational features that cause measurement or delegation to be costly. For example, it seems likely that marginal costs of delegation are lower and that resulting unsupervised allocations are of more value to customers when agents and principals are members of the same organization (because of organizational identification). By this logic, delegation costs should be lower within organizations than across organizational boundaries. Measurement should be more attractive when principal and agent are members of different organizations than when both work for the same organization. Consistent with this, Erin Anderson and David Schmittlein (1984) and Anderson (1985) show that external incentives tend to be used more often between client and contractor than between employer and employee.

There are numerous organizational and task features that affect measurement costs. Some of these are

1. *Repetitiveness of the task.* Repetitive tasks offer more opportunities for observation of all phases of the agent's work, thereby diminishing knowledge asymmetries between principal and agent. Repetitive tasks permit the use of statistical sampling techniques since each repetition can, subject to standard qualifications, be viewed as coming from the same statistical population. Thus, when tasks are repetitive, it is more likely that measurement will be inexpensive on all effort dimensions and that a situation that permits full supervision will be attained.

2. *Complexity of the task.* Oliver Williamson (1975, p. 23) notes that task complexity contributes to the costs of verifying agent performance by overtaxing the principal's cognitive capabilities. Simple tasks with few activities, thus few effort dimensions, are easier to measure than more complex tasks. Simple tasks, therefore, have greater potential to become fully supervised.

3. *Newness of the task.* Tasks that are old and well-established provide more opportunities for measurement. Older tasks have had time to be subjected to job designs that render them more measurable. Also, the principal is more likely to be familiar with all task activities. Old tasks are more likely to become fully supervised.

4. *Specialized knowledge required by the task.* Tasks that require specialized experience or training may be difficult to measure or observe because it may be difficult to find anyone (other than the agent) who is qualified to design a measurement system and interpret its results. For example, it might be impossible to establish adequate performance measures for the world's foremost heart surgeon, since much about his technique, the cases he tends to accept, and so on, are unique (and the uniqueness is what is valued; it is what makes him the world's foremost). There are similar difficulties when the task involves pushing beyond the boundaries of technology in fields other than medicine (for example, defense avionics). Full supervision is very unlikely to be achieved in such situations.

5. *Interdependence and separability of effort.* Interdependence (see Alchian and Demsetz, 1972, p. 777; Williamson, 1975, p. 83) refers to a situation in which numerous parties in a production process all have the ability to hinder others because the work being done by each is so closely related. Such processes are often sequential and adequate downstream performance requires adequate upstream performance. Performance failures are difficult to diagnose because tasks of numerous workers are so tightly coupled. Separability of effort (Alchian and Demsetz, 1972) is a related problem in which observers of work being done by a group have difficulty dis-

tinguishing how much effort each member is contributing. Tasks in such settings are inherently difficult to observe, hence full supervision of them is unlikely to be attained.

6. *Environmental covariates and noise.* This characteristic of some work settings is similar to interdependence and separability in that there are features of the setting that make it difficult to attribute specific performance to particular agents. What is different here is that the factors that also determine an individual's measured performance are not under the control of coworkers but are, rather, beyond the control of anyone in the work environment and are due to outside factors. For example, two coworkers doing the same work on different machines might produce at different rates because one machine is more reliable than the other. Or, two salesmen assigned to different regions may perform differently because of regional variations in the economy. In both of these situations, attribution of performance to individuals is made difficult by external random factors (machine reliability, regional economic variation) for which there is no measure available. Full supervision is unlikely to be attained in such a situation.

There are also numerous organizational and task features that affect delegation costs. Some of these are

1. *Organization size.* Industrial relations theory suggests that large organizations, because of the sheer number of employees, may be perceived as less personal than smaller organizations (Brody, 1980; Lee, 1987). Large organizations, therefore, may find it more difficult than small organizations to inspire organizational identification and loyalty.

2. *Whether organization is public or private.* Conventional wisdom says that employees of public bureaucracies are less motivated than those employed in the private sector. If this is true, then costs of delegation would be higher in public than in private endeavors.

3. *Cultural homogeneity of organization.* Ouchi (1981, p. 55) contends that cultural homogeneity within Japanese firms allows easier alignment of objectives between firms and their employees.[1] By this logic, organizations with a greater degree of similarity between their employees may have lower delegation costs.

4. *Duration of relationship between principal and agent.* Deming (1986, p. 35) has lobbied against the traditional practice of awarding contracts to the lowest bidder, advocating instead intimate, long-term relationships between customer and supplier. The hope is that two firms so closely linked will internalize each other's objectives to a great extent, creating the potential for greater gains from their joint activity. Delegation costs should become lower as the duration (or expected duration) of relationship between principal and agent grows.

5. *Frequency of interaction between firm employees.* March and Simon (1958, p. 67) suggest that employees are more likely to identify with a firm when there are frequent interactions with other firm members. This means that delegation costs should be lower in organizations that are less geographically dispersed, and in which the work done is less autonomous, whether because of the nature of the work or organizational custom.

---

[1] It should be noted that Ouchi does not advocate policies aimed at enforcing cultural homogenity in a workforce. He rightly points out that such policies would be blatantly discriminatory.

6. *Organizational prestige.* March and Simon (*loc. cit.*) also suggest that employees are more likely to identify with firms that are widely known and well regarded. Organizations may be considered prestigious because of their success, their size, their reputation as a good community influence, or for any of a variety of other reasons. Prestige, however arrived at, then, would reduce costs of delegation.

7. *Degree to which employee needs are met in the organization.* Organizations that more completely meet their employees' needs and desires are likely to experience lower delegation costs (March and Simon, *loc. cit.*). Included here are employees' non-material needs for companionship, quality of life, and so on. Some organizations enjoy inherent advantages in meeting the needs of their customers because of the nature of the work. Likert (1961) and others have shown that it is too simplistic to argue that satisfied employees are always productive employees, but employee satisfaction with the working environment has been found to create the potential for lower delegation costs.

8. *Perceived level of mutual commitment.* The more employees perceive that the organization has taken on responsibility for their well-being, the more loyalty employees are likely to feel to the organization; hence, lower delegation costs are likely. There is evidence, for example, that the Japanese practice of assuring employees lifetime employment greatly increases loyalty to the organization (see, for example, Rohlen, 1974).

In making recommendations, one must be attuned to more than just the overall cost of measurement. The supervisory mode that should be adopted depends not on a summary of cost of measurement like an average, but rather on how costs vary across dimensions. A task may have seven of eight measurement dimensions that are easy to measure, but the eighth might be costly enough to make measurement on that dimension inadvisable. In this situation, the appropriate supervisory mode would be partial supervision, despite the possibility that measurement costs overall could be said to be low (because average or median measurement cost is low). If even one critical dimension is too expensive to measure, then full supervision cannot be successfully attained (which provides more reason to believe that partial supervision is most common).

It is worthwhile to generate recommendations for some specific scenarios, to illustrate the potential scope of the model. For example:

1. *Pencil procurement.* Suppose one firm contracts with another for provision of a large quantity of ordinary No. 2 pencils. Since the contract spans firms, alignment between the objectives of contractor employees and the principal would not ordinarily be high. But pencils are a standard product for which production processes are repetitive and well-established. Therefore, measurement of agent activities is likely to be inexpensive on critical dimensions. This situation is characterized by high delegation costs, and strong potential for full supervision. By consulting Table 11.1, you can see that measurement is the recommended method of management.

2. *A small, private advertising agency.* A small, private advertising agency is likely to have low delegation costs precisely because it is small and private. Because advertising often succeeds to the extent that it is creative and original, full supervision is unlikely to be obtained. Measurement cost is likely to be high on some dimensions, so delegation is the preferred method of management.

3. *A small, private rivet producer.* A small, private company engaged in production of a certain type of rivet is likely to have low delegation costs

precisely because it is small and private. Because the manufacture of rivets is repetitive and well-established, measurement costs are probably also quite low here. Either measurement-based or delegatory management might work in this situation.

Chapter Twelve:

When Neither Management Method Seems Recommended

I n each of the just-discussed scenarios, the model seems to make clear recommendations. Not all situations are so simple. For example:

1. *Defense acquisition of a missile guidance system.*
   Suppose the Department of Defense hires a firm to build a missile guidance system. The product is highly complex and of unprecedented technological sophistication. Development activities are neither repetitive nor well-established. Measurement difficulties are therefore likely. Delegation costs are also high because the contract spans organizational boundaries and because the principal is a government bureaucracy. Neither management approach seems likely to work very well.

2. *Large software development firm.* Consider a large firm engaged in large-scale systems development, which is usually a complex, non-repetitive task. As in the previous example, costs of delegation are high and measurement is expensive. Again, neither management approach seems ideal.

These two scenarios correspond to the cell in Table 11.1 marked "Nothing Works." Unfortunately, as customers come to expect products with more customized features (see Leavitt, 1988, on the pluralization of consumption) and products become increasingly technologically advanced, a large and probably growing portion of important productive activity can be described as having high delegation and measurement costs. What courses of action are available to a principal in a situation that seems appropriate for neither measurement-based nor delegatory management? There are two options: She can convert the situation into one in which measurement is appropriate; or, she can convert the situation into one for which delegation is appropriate.

The first option is historically the most popular and manifests itself in the design of jobs and organizational structure. The traditional response to management difficulties is to redesign the job being done by the agent. There are several steps that can be taken to make jobs more susceptible to measurement, including:

1. *Standardization.* Almost all processes are repetitive at some level of abstraction. Although software development, for example, results in very different products that, as Frederick Brooks (1987) has noted, are not self-similar (similar segments of software are extracted into common modules or subroutines and so appear only once), the development can be said to proceed in a number of phases (for example, requirements definition, analysis, design, implementation, and maintenance). Where phases are extracted, standard methods of execution can be established. Measurements can be more easily made by noting variances from standards.

2. *Specification.* This step is closely related to standardization but deserves separate treatment because it implies something more detailed. Where standardization is the practice of deciding on appropriate product properties or worker behavior at a certain stage in a process, specification involves constructing a detailed model of

the process. Measurement is made easier because variances from specification can be noted at any point in the process, not merely at points for which standards exist. Specification is, in effect, standardization of the entire process and every step in it. Leon Osterweil (1987) advocates an extreme version of standardization to manage the software development process in a paper titled "Software Processes Are Software Too."

3. *Subdivision, functional decomposition, and regrouping.* Costs of measuring jobs that are composed of diverse and specialized activities can sometimes be reduced by dividing the job into tasks and subtasks, and grouping similar tasks and subtasks. There are several advantages to this approach. First, grouping similar activities makes repetition and self-similarity more visible within the complexity of the overall process. Second, people working on similar activities can be assigned overseers that have the same specialized knowledge as workers; accountants work for accountants, engineers for engineers, and so on. Third, if subdivision is successful, then standardization and specification can be facilitated by isolating similar aspects of jobs.

Not all development or production processes lend themselves to easy conversion to measurement appropriateness. As has been mentioned in discussing choice of supervisory mode (full, partial, or none), the degree to which measurement costs can be decreased depends not only on the ingenuity of measurers and job redesigners (for example, the principal), but also on the inherent nature of the job or task. As was noted, despite Osterweil's optimism about prospects for programming software development, some experts question the feasibility and wisdom of extensive subdivision, specification, and standardization of software development. Curtis *et al.* (1987) and M.M. Lehman (1987) submit that human processes may be too dynamic to be captured by static representations. DeMarco went even further in questioning the commonly expressed desire to render software development rotable—that is, to make the process repeatable in the sense that next steps are specified for any eventuality and such that it can be executed by rote (see Humphrey, 1989, on the virtues of repeatability in software development). DeMarco's comments relate specifically to software development but are applicable to other development and production processes:

> The idea of a software factory is a joke—that we can build software by rote—that's ridiculous. If the work is deterministic, we will do with it what we do with any other big piece of deterministic work. We'll put the deterministic work inside the computer and let the computer do the deterministic portion, leaving the person who interacts with the computer—the other half of the system—to do the work whose roteness has decreased, not increased. Every time you automate something, what's left of the person's work is less deterministic, until eventually, when you automate enough, there's no deterministic element left for the person's work—no rote. We've driven rote out of the system. . . . Little by little, the work is becoming zero-percent rotable. . . . Our work is not deterministic. It's far too inventive. We're knowledge workers, not factory workers.

DeMarco argues that there are certain jobs and certain aspects of jobs that resist redesign by subdivision, specification, and standardization. Ishikawa (1985) lists similar redesign limitations. Such jobs, and tasks within jobs, are characterized by non-repeatability, unprecedentedness, interdependencies, inseparabilities, cognitive complexity, and inherent knowledge asymmetries—in short, by factors that cause observational difficulties.

The degree to which the end products of a production process are customized also figures greatly in determining whether the process can be easily redesigned to be more appropriate for measurement. Customization implies less than perfect similarity between consecutive outputs of the production process. Less similarity between products implies less similarity between steps in the production process—making one product different from another requires doing something different during production. The process may still be repeatable at some level of abstraction.

For example, at an abstract level, a journalist performs the same steps over and over: 1) acquire lead, 2) research lead, 3) write story, 4) submit story to editor, 6) revise, and 7) submit final copy. But in reality, every story is different and requires different actions and the exercise of considerable discretion in carrying out each of the steps. Similarly, a physician repeats steps in a process: 1) greet patient, 2) diagnose ailment, and 3) prescribe cure. But every patient's case is different and should be regarded as different if the quality of the job is to be maintained.

Journalism, general practice medicine, and software development, all of which generate customized products, may be repeatable in some sense, but they are not repeatable in the sense of the idealized factory process. The latter requires repetition of very self-similar steps; the former do not. The difference is one of degree, but it has important implications for ease and even feasibility of measurement. In journalism or medicine or software development, it is not clear how to compare what is measured on any single production cycle with anything else. There are always things that can be counted, but for these customizing jobs it is unclear how to interpret what is counted. In such processes, non-repetitiveness is an *essential* property of the task. Most of the value is added to the product in non-repetitive activities; non-repetitiveness cannot and should not be driven out of the process.

The second option available to the principal when a job seems inappropriate for either style of management is converting the situation into one more suitable to delegation. This sort of conversion can also be effected in various ways, including

1. *Promoting organizational intimacy.* Ouchi (1981, p. 9) proposes strengthening the potential for commitment to an organization by any means that promote intimacy. Among the actions that can be taken are reorganizations that make hierarchies flatter or work groups smaller. Work spaces can be reconfigured to promote casual contact

between employees and between managers and workers who need to work together.

2. *Promoting trust.* Steps taken to make employers and employees more trustful of each other can also lower delegation costs. Examples of such steps might include forming long-term commitments between firm and employees (such as promises of lifetime employment), or intentionally introducing mutual vulnerabilities into the relationship so that each party is, to some extent, at the other's mercy. Employee trust can also be increased by investments that suggest permanence of the employee base; for example, it has been suggested that firms that invest heavily in employee training gain loyalty along with enhanced employee capabilities (see "Musical Chairs," *The Economist,* July 17, 1993, p. 67).

3. *Better leadership.* Effective appeals to sentiment or especially skillful expression of a vision can also be useful in lowering delegation costs. Managers can be trained in management styles that emphasize inspiring and trusting employees rather than analyzing and coercing them.

Just as redesign for measurement may be difficult in some situations, so may reduction of delegation costs. Delegation costs are more under the control of an organization's managers than measurement costs are because managers determine their own behavior toward workers, which, in turn, largely determines delegation costs. Nevertheless, delegation can be difficult to implement. Delegatory management is a subtle matter. None of the steps just suggested to reduce delegation costs necessarily works; if, for whatever reason, workers regard the employer's gestures toward delegation as less than sincere, delegation costs may even increase in response. Managers lacking the intangible elements of personality often called leadership skills may have difficulty in lowering delegation costs. A history of distrust between the employer and employees, or even one event that was interpreted cynically by workers, can impede the establishment of delegatory management styles. Moreover, conditions that allow delegation costs to remain low are fragile; the tentative balance of factors that allows delegation is easily disturbed by awkward or seemingly disingenuous actions by even one member of the organization's management team. Since trust and commitment are often slow to evolve, delegatory styles of measurement also take longer to establish than measurement-based styles.

Measurement versus Delegation in Real Organizations

The two management styles have strengths and weaknesses relative to each other. Measurement is relatively easy to implement. There is nothing subtle about using carrots and sticks. Steps taken to set up a measurement system are tangible and easy to defend using words such as "accountability." Job redesigns to lower measurement costs are also tangible and easily visible. Standardizing, specifying, and subdividing seem scientific in the Taylorist sense and have a history of working well in manufacturing. Factory analogies are attractive because of the success of mass production in the early part of this century.

On the other hand, often the best that can be managed through measurement, even after job redesign, is partial supervision, which generates relatively weak improvements in value to the customer compared to delegation or full supervision, both of which move the agent's effort allocation at least some distance along the best-mix path. In addition, partial supervision produces significant distortion of incentives. If motivation theorists are correct in their conclusions, distorted incentives obscure inclinations the agent may have toward doing the job right for internal reasons, like pride in his work. Worse, if targets are set badly, distortion may become significant enough to produce dysfunction. Furthermore, when customer preferences change, the incentive system has to be redesigned and adjusted; if the customer changes preferences often, the incentive system is likely to lag behind the customer's true preferences. As Ishikawa (1985) observes of production processes: "Conditions change constantly, and the commands given by superiors can never catch up with changing conditions" (p. 66).

In contrast, delegation cannot produce distortion. If the customer's value function changes, the change is immediately reflected in the effort allocation of the agent, as long as he is aware of the change. When delegation costs are low, value is produced efficiently since agent effort allocations always follow the best-mix path. Under delegation, workers are likely to take more initiative; they act in accordance with their own expectations instead of reacting to whatever carrot hangs before them. As Ishikawa notes, given a chance, "experience and skill [can] make up for inadequacies in standards and regulations" (*loc. cit.*).

Delegation is subtle and difficult to establish. It takes a long time to begin working and is easily dislodged. The steps taken to establish delegation are intangible and have short-term costs without obvious short-term benefits. Thus, delegatory styles are often difficult to defend. Placing trust in employees may seem as if no one is minding the store if things go wrong. Creating vulnerabilities, mutual or otherwise, may not seem to be a good idea from some perspectives. Reorganization intended to promote intimacy rarely yields quantifiable cost savings unless it also significantly reduces headcount—and reducing headcount may result in bad feelings among employees that offset advantages due to increased intimacy.

On the whole, however, the recommendations that can be generated for specific scenarios give the impression that delegation is underused—perhaps drastically so—in real settings. Some very common measurement-based practices seem curiously inappropriate for their settings. For example, Management-By-Objectives, or MBO (Drucker, 1954), as it is often practiced, seems especially misguided. MBO prescribes setting objectives, establishing quantitative criteria for measuring progress, and linking rewards with achievement as indicated by the measurements. The practice of MBO is obviously a form of measurement-based management, but it is mostly used in managerial and professional settings where tasks are not well-suited to measurement. For similar reasons, merit-based pay systems that depend on measurable criteria for success also seem badly conceived, despite their growing popularity. The same holds for third-party audits intended to enhance organizational capability, including the Malcolm Baldrige Quality Award, ISO 9000 certification, and Software Capability Evaluations. (There is more on this in Chapter Seventeen.)

Some measurement experts and management theorists agree that measurement-based management is often used in inappropriate settings. Tilford commented on MBO:

> I was fairly high-level management of a very large company, . . . and I was under an MBO system for a while. . . . the MBO systems that I was under, however humanely they were handled, never added to my capabilities. . . . frequently, they got in the way of making a really good decision for the company. What they did do is, they gave me good indications of how to make decisions that would optimize well for me, or my boss. . . . So, here I am. I've got an MBO system on me, and my boss has got one on him, and so forth. And I'm coming toward the end of the year, and I've got to make a decision about bringing some training in for a project that's going to start right after the fiscal year. I know from experience that the sooner I do this the better, and so I put in a request to call for training. Maybe it's a twenty-thousand dollar expenditure for training for someone to come in and teach layered virtual machine design. . . . I submit it to my boss, and my boss says, "I'll sign this, but let's just hold the paperwork. We'll act on it after the first. That way it won't get us over this year's budget. Because if it does, you won't make your financial piece on your MBO, then you won't get your bonus, and then I won't get mine." Some kinds of decisions like that were made.

The distorting influences of measurement in this account are exactly as suggested by the model and are central to Tilford's concerns about MBO. DeMarco cites Deming on the same point. Deming is a vocal critic of MBO, performance evaluation, the Baldrige Award, and other systems of external evaluation. In the words of DeMarco:

> Third-party assessment through metrics is, I think, a
> mistake even in a less knowledge-worker environ-
> ment [than software development]. Deming's point
> twelve of the Fourteen Points says, Chuck out your
> annual employee review and your salary incentives.
> Get rid of all of that stuff.[1]

As a professional activity that has much mental content and is not
very rotable, software development seems particularly poorly
suited to measurement-based management. Brooks (1987) lists
characteristics of software that make its production difficult and
also contribute to observational difficulties. Software is not self-
similar. Software is complex and its complexity is arbitrary and
idiosyncratic, "forced without rhyme or reason by the many
human institutions and systems to which . . . interfaces must conform." It is "pure thought-stuff, infinitely malleable." It is invisi-
ble and "has no ready geometric representation in the way that
land has maps, silicon chips have diagrams, computers have con-
nectivity schematics." Its design requires creativity and is characterized by asymmetries of knowledge; as Curtis *et al.* (1988) also
document, there are huge individual differences between programmers and between designers.

There is evidence that software development is plagued by
measurement dysfunction. DeMarco described what he maintains is a common scenario:

> . . . people who are reluctant to upset management
> are very inclined to bill their work in a given week
> not to the task that they were really doing—because
> that was getting dangerously close to full—but to
> some similar task. . . . differentiation between tasks . . .
> is negligible . . . if that task happens to be less full
> than the other one, [the person will] bill to an empty

---

[1] A reading of Deming's Fourteen Points reveals that his advice *is* this
unequivocal. The discomfort that many managers and consultants feel in
response to such direct criticism of cherished notions of external motivation
(for example, MBO and other performance evaluation systems) is apparent
from reading books *about* Deming's methods but not *by* Deming himself. In
these secondhand accounts, point 12 is often diluted considerably in strained
attempts to make Deming's message more palatable.

> task, so what happens is that none of them fills up
> until they all fill up. . . . people will always stuff the
> time they spent on a given task into a related task in
> order not to call attention to the manager of his or
> her failure.

Putnam mentioned how counting lines of code (LOCs) for use in deriving developer or organizational productivity measures (for example, lines of code per person-day) results in artificially lengthened code. Card surmised that there is more behavior of this nature in software development than is ever discovered or admitted.

Interestingly, however, there is great enthusiasm for measurement among software development thinkers. Barry Boehm (1981), an influential voice in the software metrics community, explicitly endorses using MBO in software development. The Goal-Question-Metric (GQM) framework of Victor Basili and D.M. Weiss (1984) is currently fashionable in software metrics circles but seems destined to propagate dysfunction according to the model presented in this book. The GQM approach advocates measurement of high-profile areas associated with organizational goals but is not concerned with making measures comprehensive. Grady and Caswell (1987), in their influential book about software measurement, encourage setting aside difficult-to-measure dimensions of performance and focusing on what can be easily measured—a recipe for dysfunction according to my model.

Tilford expresses the central distinction between measurement-based and delegatory management in a way that makes clear the advantages of using delegation in many situations where measurement is often used. He says "management" instead of "measurement" and "leading" instead of "delegation," but his meaning is quite consistent with the recommendation to expand use of delegatory styles of management:

> . . . my favorite view of the distinction between man-
> agement and leading is really one that can be stated
> very simply: You manage things, and you lead peo-
> ple. You control things, and you release people.

DeMarco makes a similar point about control-oriented management methods:

> More harm than good is done in the name of control. The best thing you can do on a project is to get on top of an absolutely out-of-control team that's headed in the right direction. . . . you can't steer it, you can't make it go faster or slower, but it is making tremendous progress.

Insight into the advantages of relaxing external monitoring and incentives can be extracted from a seemingly unrelated field—dramatic theory. A tenet of theater, according to Lee Devin (1983), is that the vitality and spontaneity of a good play arise from intentionally *not* repeating exactly the same motions in each rendition. Even though a play is among the most repetitive of processes on paper—the words on the page do not vary between readings—the best plays vary considerably in performance as actors interact. One word spoken with different inflection prompts other actors to improvise in the manner and timing of response, which in turn results in further use of discretion, always within the rigorous framework of the play. Once something is changed at a point during the play, what is appropriate thereafter also changes. Devin claims that there are two types of control often attempted in the theater, which he describes metaphorically: 1) the sort that one uses when placing an object gripped firmly in the hand exactly where one wants it; and 2) the sort that calls for releasing the object from some height and trusting gravity and future actions to bring it to rest where intended. The latter sort of control—in the theater or in the production of goods or services—seems to have much to recommend it.

Chapter Thirteen:
Purely Informational Measurement

"Where we go astray is when we start trying to measure people. If we could figure out how to decouple [the] measurement system [from motivation] so it is truly just [measuring] things, . . . if we could figure out how to do that, then I think it would be tremendously successful. I don't know the answer to that. I wish I did. I'd sure give it away."

In the above quote, Tilford wishes for a practical distinction to parallel the conceptual difference between motivational and informational uses of measurement. If the decoupling could be achieved, there would be obvious benefits. Information conveyed by an agent who is not worried about how the information will affect his future rewards might provide accurate warning of production problems or exact insight into processes that would allow major improvements. In the words of Expert X, measures would provide "a quantitative way to have insight." All of the interviewed experts cited such informational benefits as justifications for measurement programs.

Organizations that seek to use measurement purely informationally are not common. Most users of organizational measurements are not in this category, even if they are inclined to claim that they are. Most will admit motivational aims if pressed, or at least make statements that casually mingle the two intentions.

For example, one expert interviewed for this book expressed the goals of the measurement systems he had helped design in informational terms; but, later in his interview, he added that "managers are and should be held accountable for the performance of their projects, and that should be reported and measured." The tendency of measurement system architects to invoke motivational *and* informational intentions is but one factor that makes pure informational measurement difficult to achieve.

As Tilford implies in the passage at the beginning of this section, there is reason to question whether the two intended uses of measurement *can* be decoupled in real settings. People tend to react to the fact and form of measurement when they know about it. Measurement cannot easily be hidden for most production processes, nor is it often desirable to hide measurement. As was discussed in Chapter Three, the principal has little to say about how the agent interprets the measurement system. The agent is ultimately free to interpret and react to the system in whatever way he chooses. In cases where purely informational measurement is realized, it often reverts to having motivational features after a short period of time.

The consequences that arise when informational measurement turns motivational are by now familiar. Workers manage the flow of information, undermining its accuracy. There are no warning signs of problems on the way—employees conceal those. Instead, there are unpleasant surprises that happen when a problem becomes so serious that it cannot be concealed by workers close to it. Organizational quasi-experiments are compromised because measurement instruments provide biased readings. Learning is at least imperfect, and possibly nonexistent, as managers believe the biased measurements and draw from them inferences that are, at best, not quite right, and at worst, completely at odds with reality.

It is important to note that these problems can arise only in situations where measures do not span all critical dimensions. When all critical dimensions are measured (that is, full supervision), true performance is revealed. In such a situation, the agent has no latitude to manage appearances because all of the important aspects of his performance can be observed. The same measures that accurately motivate also accurately convey information. This is yet another reason that full supervision is desirable. Much enthusiasm about measurement in organizations is probably based on a vision of this ideal state where true output is known, incentives are perfectly aligned, and measurement information accurately portrays reality. As has been argued, however, full supervision can rarely be realized.[1]

When there is potential for subversion of the measurement system, the agent must be prevented from reacting to the measurement system to preserve the accuracy of the information it conveys. This is precisely the opposite of what was intended in motivational measurement. In motivational measurement, part of the cost to the principal is for making targets meaningful—that is, worth reacting to—for the agent.

In informational measurement, the principal should instead try to make the upper limits of measurement systems seem inconsequential to the agent. There are several possible ways of doing this. The principal can try to manage the agent's perceptions of the measurement system. More specifically, the principal can try to convince the agent that his prospects for future rewards are not at all dependent on the measurements. But, as March and Simon

---

[1] The informational benefits of measuring dimensions that would yield full supervision must be incorporated into the marginal cost calculations involved in deciding whether to measure a particular dimension (see Chapter Eight). It is possible that a dimension not worth measuring from a purely motivational standpoint will be worth measuring when informational benefits are taken into account, especially if there are one or very few difficult-to-measure critical dimensions. Imagine, for example, a situation in which there are two effort dimensions, one easy to measure, one difficult to measure. Suppose also that partial supervision is recommended by the motivational model in Chapters Five through Nine. The motivational model does not, however, take into account the informational benefits of having a perfectly accurate measurement system—the consequent ability to reliably learn about and perhaps dramatically improve the process, for example. Taking the informational benefits into account might make it worthwhile to pay the cost of full supervision. Notice, however, that this eventuality requires two special circumstances: that the marginal cost of measuring on the hard-to-measure dimension is not drastically higher than the marginal value provided according to the motivational calculation; and that accurate information about the organizational process is quite valuable—that there is great, rather than incremental, potential for learning about and improving the process in question.

(1958) observe, workers in real organizations are notoriously cynical about declarations to this effect. They know that the rate at which widgets, interviews, or lines of code are produced does matter. All else being equal, faster production is preferable to slower production. Workers expect, then, that rewards will go to the speedy. Denying the obvious is unlikely to be of help to the principal.

When the benefits associated with the direction of a particular measure are obvious (such as high quantity or low defect rates), agents become sensitive to a competitive dynamic that is not represented in models that feature one principal and one agent. As agents become familiar with the system of measurement and discover ways to exploit it, they realize that their coworkers are also discovering the means of exploitation. A dilemma arises. If coworkers do not exploit the system, then a given worker will benefit from exploiting the system because he will look better by measured criteria than his more honest coworkers. If coworkers do exploit the system, the given worker will still benefit from exploiting the system since he will not seem to lag behind his less honest coworkers. This logic applies to all workers in the group. Exploiting the system is, then, a dominating strategy for all workers.

The dilemma can be affected by any change that de-emphasizes competition between workers. For example, workers might be promoted in lockstep, at least up to a certain level in the organization. Promoting people over a longer time horizon might somewhat mitigate the benefits of distinguishing oneself from peers, because rewards are heavily discounted when they are far in the future and because any one measurement is of less importance when the evaluation period is long. Ouchi (1981) notes that the employment practices of Japanese firms are designed in just this manner, to reduce competition between coworkers. Interestingly, many firms in the West are moving in the opposite direction, toward merit-based systems of compensation (Tully, 1993). Western firms' fondness for merit-based systems is partly due to historical trends that are difficult to reverse. If a Western company announced a program of promoting people very slowly and in lockstep, many employees would probably seek employment elsewhere.[2] Also, in industries in which there is a scarcity of people with particular skill sets, demand for the skill set may intervene to force rewards to be allocated sooner and less evenly across individuals.

There are also procedural means that can be used to make measurement more purely informational. In particular, the practice of *aggregation* of measurements makes motivational measurement impossible. When measurements are aggregated, members of an organizational hierarchy can view measurements only at their own level or higher. For example, if Bob and Fred work for Susan, Bob and Fred get to see their own measurements but Susan is permitted to look at only the aggregation of Bob's and Fred's measurements. She cannot get information that would allow her to determine how Bob's measurements compare to Fred's. Bob and Fred can assess their own performance because they each know their individual number and the average for their peers. Because they know that Susan cannot see individual information, Bob and Fred have no reason to manage the flow of information upward. The same holds all the way to the top of a hierarchy.

Card, DeMarco, Tilford, and John Musa argued that aggregation or an equally strong procedural method is important to the success of a measurement program. Musa commented that a policy dictating how measurement information was to be used would be adequate to enforce aggregation. DeMarco advocated a stronger method:

> . . . it's not enough to set the data up with a promise. I mean that the data has to be kept by individuals. The individual promises that he's going to keep the data. I mean, I go to you if I'm the measurer and I say, "Look, I'm going to do this, and I'm not going to take the data and put it in a company database. I'll keep it at home, and if I get fired, I'll take it with me."

---

[2] The reasons for this fundamental difference are complex, based in culture and history. See Thomas Rohlen (1974) for an anthropological treatment of these differences.

Although it may seem extreme, DeMarco's method is more able to diffuse the dilemma just discussed. Musa's policy-based aggregation approach is vulnerable to what has been called a loose-cannon problem (Larkey and Caulkins, 1992). Even if measures are being aggregated, workers have incentives to exploit the measurement system if they suspect that the measures will ever be disaggregated. If there is potential for a new manager who does not agree with the philosophy of aggregation (a loose cannon) to reach a position of authority in the organization, workers will be best off if they have been exploiting the system all along. Alternatively, a manager may simply change her mind about a policy of aggregation. Jones mentioned a situation in which one division of a company was sold and began operating with completely different managers who dramatically changed the company's approach to measurement. Paulish conceded that it is impossible to control what managers do with measurement information once they have it; and that managers may be tempted to do secretly other than what was agreed on or admitted publicly. As long as possibilities like these loom in workers' minds, the incentive to exploit a measurement system remains. The implication is that only methods of data collection and retention that make disaggregation impossible, like the one proposed by DeMarco, can completely abate the temptation to undermine an informational system of measurement. DeMarco emphasizes the seriousness of the loose-cannon problem in a grim example:

> It could be like the end of the Weimar Republic. . . .
> The Weimar Republic had collected all kinds of data
> about names, addresses, and religions of people.
> They knew where all the Jews were, and the census
> data was put to use . . . by the Nazis.

Tilford told a story that dramatically illustrates the damage that can be done to an informational measurement program when even the best intentioned loose cannon takes even the subtlest action:

> The biggest disaster I have ever witnessed was actu-
> ally, in the beginning, a high success. It was . . .

around four- to five-hundred people who basically were in the maintenance business for a huge operating system. And they finally, after years and years and years of management trying to get them to report and count errors, agreed to do it. And they were doing it, and a lot of information was coming out of it. They were putting it up on the walls, and people were looking at it, and people were making decisions around all kinds of issues because of being able to see these things. Then, one day, a very high-level president, a president of this company—big company—was taken through the hall . . . and he saw the [wall charts] and he said, "What's this all about?" So they told him, and he said, "This is wonderful," and he took out a red pen—he had one— and he circled [one group's numbers] . . . and he wrote there "great work" and wrote his name down. . . . He put the pen away and walked off. And literally the next day, all of the graphs came off the walls. No one ever put any graphs up again. . . . Management said, "Put those graphs back up. Don't worry about them. We apologize. . . . You must put these graphs back up." Nobody did. What are you going to do, fire them all?

In a sense, this organization was lucky in that employees abandoned the measurement system so overtly. Covert abandonment of the system would have been much more destructive. Graphs might have been left on the wall but could have become meaningless as employees quietly conspired to undermine their informational content. Several experts mentioned the danger of this sort of quiet non-compliance in their interviews. Quiet non-compliance is worse than the more visible variety because the former conveys the impression to managers that they are seeing things as they really are. The quiet subversion of a measurement system can also be worse than no system of measurement at all. With no system, managers do not know what is happening, and they know that they do not know. With a quietly subverted system, managers still do not know what is happening, but they think they do. They make decisions, therefore, about process improvements and the like based on faulty information.[3] Ironically, this sort of measurement has the opposite of its intended effect. Introduced to provide a clearer picture of what is happening in the organization, it instead creates layers of subterfuge and intrigue that vastly complicate learning about the organization. Long-term damage is done; by creating a situation in which workers feel compelled to resort to deception (whether overt or in the less sinister form of, say, unwarranted optimism), measurement designers have driven a wedge between managers and workers. With the wedge in place, measurers must doubt the accuracy of all future information coming from workers.

Despite the vulnerability to exploitation of systems that do not use strong methods like strict aggregation to protect informational integrity, strong methods are unpalatable to many managers. Mainly, this is because measurement under aggregation, or a similar procedure, constitutes a changed conception of measurement. Measurement under aggregation is no longer a way to see how subordinates are doing compared to each other. It is not a way for managers to isolate problems to a segment of the production process (production workers *can* use the information in this way). Indeed, much of the managerial diagnostic capability envisioned by many advocates of measurement is lost when a manager cannot see the measurements corresponding to different areas within her responsibility. What managers have instead is a self-assessment tool. The system tells them how they are doing at all times compared to their peers—and that is all it tells them. Pinpointing and gaining understanding of particular problems requires venturing out into direct contact with the production environment, communicating openly with subordinates who must come to view their supervisor as someone to help them solve problems. The workers do most of the analytic and process redesign work that managers considered their job before aggregation began. The emphasis of the manager's job shifts from analysis and evaluation to inspiration, communication, and provision

---

[3] Or, as the late, great Satchel Paige is said to have put it, "It ain't what you don't know that gets you in trouble; it's what you think you know that just ain't so."

of assistance for the subordinates who do the real work and who also analyze and improve their own processes. What the purveyors of analogies between cockpit instruments and measurement systems tend to overlook is that pilots rely heavily on cockpit instruments only in rare circumstances and as a last resort; in most cases, a pilot gains the crucial moment-to-moment operational information he uses to fly the plane from more direct sensory experiences—his view out the window, the feel of the steering mechanism, and interaction with other crew members.[4]

Two experts interviewed for this study expressed the view that self-assessment is the eventual endpoint of a successful measurement program. Card stated his goal in modest terms:

> My real goal is to get people to collect and use data themselves. . . . the real goal is to get them to use data themselves practically. . . .

DeMarco was more emphatic:

> The individual doesn't misuse metrics. . . . I give you some way to assess your own ability and compare it to an average—averages across the board of the whole organization—and you find you are very weak in testing. . . . your every inclination is to do something about it. You get yourself trained, or you get yourself out of that business, or you leave the field entirely. Those are the things the manager would do if he got to know the data. Since you are going to do them anyway, the manager doesn't really need to know the data. I think a more important thing is to get the data to the individual who really cares. People want to do a good job. If you know you're not good at something, you want to get better at it, or not do it. . . . I go to you and say, "If you help me, I will show you how to collect data for yourself

---

[4] Pilots and organization leaders may also have in common that at any given time there is probably nothing directly in front of them to be run into; thus, doing nothing is rarely cataclysmic for pilots or managers.

about your own set process and we'll show you how to compare yourself to the averages I've established doing the same thing for other people. I'm not going to share the data with anyone, just like the company doctor doesn't share information with the insurance company." . . . I don't give the data to the manager. The manager never knows who's doing what, but the manager doesn't care, because if you're learning, and you're doing something about it, everybody's a winner.

Although informational measurement enforced by strong safeguards is antithetical to motivational measurement, it is entirely consistent with delegatory modes of control. From this perspective, the ideal to which organizations should usually aspire is one in which workers are internally motivated and measurement provides them with self-assessment information. Measurement and motivation are decoupled. Managers are transformed—some would say reduced—to communicating direction and providing help to workers. The challenge for managers is to become more trusting, able to inspire and communicate, and willing to help rather than be helped.

Chapter Fourteen:

How Dysfunction Arises and Persists

The previous several chapters examined how principals *should* design measurement systems for particular settings. But in instances of dysfunction, principals do not act in accordance with recommendations. What can be concluded from this observation?

The economic tradition seeks to explain behavior as the joint outcome of concurrent optimization by all involved parties. Observed phenomena are the effects of optimal actions; the challenge for the scientist of this tradition is to discover an optimizing model that rationalizes the observed phenomena. There is no difference between what *should be* and what *is*, because action-takers always do what they should.[1] Therefore, if the predictions of a

---

[1] While this is an accurate depiction of how much of modern economic theorizing is conducted, it omits the arguments used to justify this practice. Milton Friedman (1953) argues persuasively that all models rely on inherently unrealistic assumptions, even those that are very useful. For example, Newton's laws governing falling bodies are useful even when the assumption that the body is falling in a vacuum is not realistic. Usefulness in prediction is, according to Friedman, the true test of a theory, and simple models that make "as if" assumptions (such as the falling body will behave "as if" in a vacuum) can do very well by this criterion. The assumption of mutual optimization by involved parties can be considered just such an "as if" assumption. Friedman

model are at variance with what is observed, then the model must be badly formulated. One conclusion that might be drawn from the observation that principals do not do what they should, according to the model in the previous chapters, is that the formulation of the model is incomplete or in error.

Scientists in behavioral traditions are troubled by the assumptions of the economic tradition, which imply that people always try to optimize, always know how to optimize, and make no mistakes in optimizing that are significant enough to impact enduringly on observed phenomena. Systematic biases, habitual mistakes—any deviations from shrewd rational behavior—are incompatible with the economic perspective. Thus, behavioral scientists might reach a different conclusion: that human limitations make the model's recommendations difficult to implement in real situations. Departures from the optimizing ideal are a determining factor in the phenomena that result. There are aspects of situations in which dysfunction occurs that cause real people to make mistakes that significantly and enduringly influence observed phenomena. There *is* a difference between what should be and what is. Any model that only tells you what you should do does not tell the whole story. The rest of the story is an explanation of the behavior that results when people make the mistakes to which they are prone while trying to do what they should.

The next two chapters seek to explain the actions of principals when they design organizational control systems that are inadequate or dysfunctional. The explanation has two flavors: The first might be called an "earnest explanation," in which the designers of the measurement system are assumed to be genuine-

---

also invokes an evolutionary argument in support of the mutual optimization assumption, contending that nature selects those who succeed best at optimizing, thus non-optimizing action can be neglected in the long term.

But, as Joseph Kadane and Larkey (1982) emphasize, the appeal of an action derived from a model of mutual optimization is crucially dependent on the mutualness of the optimization. The optimal response to a non-optimal action is not necessarily the same as the optimal response to an optimal action. Furthermore, as Keynes once pointed out, "In the long run, we are all dead." Friedman's long-run evolutionary argument in favor of ignoring non-optimal activity is of little comfort to an individual or business struggling to survive in the face of short-term non-optimizing behavior.

ly attempting to accomplish stated objectives of the organization and failing because of human limitations; the second, a more "cynical explanation," assumes guile on the part of the principals who cause dysfunction. The persistence of dysfunction is shown to be supported by self-interested behavior.

The Earnest Explanation of Dysfunction: A Systematic Error by the Principal

The mistake made by earnest measurement system designers can be simply stated in the terms of the model in previous chapters: A principal who commits dysfunctional acts mistakenly believes she is in a fully supervised situation when she is, in fact, in a partially supervised situation. In real settings, the principal has difficulty distinguishing between full and partial supervision. Sometimes, the mistake is explicit, as when a principal does not admit failure after an unsuccessful attempt to make a measurement system comprehensive. Other times, the mistake is implicit, as when a principal does not fully understand the importance of comprehensive measurement. Confusion about how measurement operates is common and is frequently inspired by idealized notions of organizational control processes based on persuasive but flawed metaphors and analogies.

How the mistake produces dysfunction should be clear. When a principal believes that full supervision has been realized, she does not worry about dysfunction, which is impossible under full supervision. Furthermore, in full supervision, it makes sense to encourage agents to maximize their performance on all measured dimensions; an increase on any measured dimension increases value to the customer when all critical dimensions are measured. In sharp contrast, making agents maximize under partial supervision results in dysfunction. As the agent extends his allocations to higher levels along the measured dimension, value first increases. Eventually, though, value begins to decrease as the agent begins to shift effort from unmeasured to measured dimensions. Thus, the difference between full and partial supervision is crucial in that prescriptions for successful principal behavior in the two cases are contradictory.

There are two ways a principal might be able to distinguish between full and partial supervision: The first is casual observation. In the employment office situation investigated by Blau (1963), it should have been obvious that important aspects of performance were not being measured. The same should be true of many professional environments. But mistakes were made in the Blau case and mistakes continue to be made in equally obvious cases. Explanation of the mistakes in such cases must resort to the psychology of sunk costs (see, for example, Dawes, 1988) and commitment to lost causes (Staw, 1982).

A second way of distinguishing full and partial supervision hinges on an inference problem. The principal sees a stream of outcomes over time that result from the interaction of her organizational control system with the environment. In a software development organization, for example, there is periodic feedback from customers about how well a computer system is performing. The feedback is noisy (in the statistical sense), occurs at irregular intervals, and may vary over time. But if full and partial supervision produce different outcomes (and the model in previous chapters suggests that they do), then the principal should eventually be able to tell, based on outcome feedback, which mode of supervision is being realized. If partial supervision is being realized, gains signaled by customer feedback should be more modest than they would be under full supervision, and dysfunction should eventually appear. The noisy, irregular, and time-dependent nature of the feedback suggests the beginnings of an explanation of why the principal often fails to distinguish between modes of supervision by solving the inference problem.

Misguided Reflexes, Folly, and the Mystique of Quantity

Casual observation fails to prevent dysfunction when principals hold fast to their own measurement system designs despite glaring problems. In real settings, principals are charged with controlling activity in their areas of organizational responsibility. Unfortunately, the need for control is often interpreted narrowly as a need for measurement-based control. The principal's job is then usually perceived to be the redesign of agent tasks to make them more measurable. The inclination to interpret control narrowly is due to what might be called a *standardization reflex*.

Since the latter part of the nineteenth century, institutions of governance have taken on a very similar form, which is hierarchical and functionally organized. There are a variety of explanations for this (see, for example, Chandler, 1977; Williamson, 1975), but one factor almost always mentioned is that this organizational form seems particularly appropriate for achieving job standardization, specification, and subdivision as described in Chapter Twelve. Huge productivity gains have resulted. A reflexive tendency toward standardizing, specifying, subdividing, and measuring that evolved from refining mass production processes is apparent in today's organizations, and in many circumstances it is still profitable.

The standardization reflex is obviously aimed at converting tasks to make them more measurement-appropriate. Given historical precedent, modern principals can hardly be faulted for assuming that conversion for measurement is the job that they have been commissioned to do. In terms of this book's model, the principal believes she is charged with the redesign of agent tasks so that measurement costs are lowered and full supervision can be gainfully realized. As has been shown, however, the standardization reflex does not always serve organizations well. The value added to some products by customization of its components is appreciable. Redesigns for measurement tend to fail when the setting and product are not particularly suited to measurement. A situation that results from a failed attempt at conversion would still require partial supervision. It is at this point that casual observation might be invoked to reveal that full supervision has *not* been realized.

A real principal may not always acknowledge that this sort of failure has occurred, however. She may prefer to believe that the job she oversees has been converted into one in which all critical effort dimensions can be measured at low cost and full supervision can be achieved—that is, that the task she believes she has been assigned has been accomplished successfully. If she defines control narrowly, as measurement-based control, and believes her job is control, failure to achieve full supervision can lead to threatening insecurities. DeMarco spoke of the insecurities faced by modern managers where control of their respective organizations is concerned:

> My father was a factory manager, maybe your father
> was a factory manager, most of us had industrial-
> revolution fathers who were managers. . . . they
> maintained a degree of control and had a meaningful
> kind of hierarchy where they gave orders and people
> followed orders, and that has been brought home to
> us by our fathers rather strongly. . . . When I tell my
> dad about riding herd on a team of programmers
> who are prima donnas, undirectable, sometimes
> flaky, sometimes brilliant, he just rolls his eyes and
> he says, "You're not a real manager. A real manager
> gives orders and the orders are followed."

Barry Staw (1982) studies "escalation situations" in which deci-
sion-makers remain committed to a course of action that has been
shown to be unproductive. Barbara Tuchman (1984), a historian,
notes the role played by what she calls "folly" in numerous historical events; she defines folly as adherence to a course of action
that could reasonably be seen to be contrary to the interests of the
action-taker (for example, why did the citizens of Troy move the
Trojan horse inside the city's walls when more prudent options
were available?). Both Staw and Tuchman have observed that
commitment to failed courses of action can arise from unwilling-
ness to admit failure, even when the task that was taken on was
impossible to complete satisfactorily.

In some cases, the principal is guilty not of refusing to face
reality but rather of super-zealousness or unclear thinking about
measurement. When this sort of difficulty arises, it is often the
result of an impressionable principal embracing rhetorically persuasive but flawed analogies. Examples of such analogies were
given in Chapter Three (for example, Kaplan and Norton's airplane cockpit discussion). Analogies to physical control systems
are so compelling to some commentators that they have based
their measurement philosophies on the analogies. The Software
Productivity Consortium's *Software Measurement Guidebook* (1992),
the writing of which was sponsored by the U.S. Defense
Advanced Research Projects Agency (DARPA), provides a case in
point:

An example of a closed loop feedback control system is a thermostatically controlled heating system. The thermostat is set to a certain "set point" temperature, which is the input goal. The thermostat controls the process, which is the heater. The heat output is monitored by a temperature measuring device that is continuously compared to the set-point goal. The thermostat uses the temperature measurement to determine if the heater should be on or off. The thermostat will turn the heater on for a temperature lower than the set point and off otherwise. Uncertainty can exist in the system in establishing the set point according to uncertain temperature requirements. Also, the temperature-measuring device may be inaccurate. However, the system's operation can be improved by ascertaining the temperature requirements and servicing the thermometer so that the system will ultimately maintain an acceptable set-point goal temperature. . . .

The [Quantitative Software Management] closed loop feedback control model represents the software process with emphasis on measurement through a holistic approach. The process is treated as a "black box" system with interest focused on the inputs and outputs at the interfaces to the system. Process and product goals are established based on the best estimates available. The process is initiated and, at the planned times, measurements are collected and analyzed and compared to measurement goals. The goals correspond to the set-point inputs and the measurements correspond to the outputs of the feedback control system. The measurements quantify the combined effect of the operation of the process and its uncertainties. These are the actual performance results. The difference between the goal and the measurements is the process variance that becomes the driver of the process correction (pp. 2–3).

The problems with this kind of analogy should, by now, be obvious. The sins committed here are, however, so grievous that they deserve to be highlighted. The process is treated as a black-box mechanism, rather than as an organizational system composed of "purposeful subsystems with their own goals" (Ackoff, 1971, p. 671). Comparison of measurements with what is expected is an explicit part of the system, guaranteeing that agents will have an incentive to corrupt measurements. Driving out differences between measured performance and desired measurements is the purpose of the system, which means agents are being encouraged—perhaps, in their view, obliged—to subvert the system. Output measurements are dangerously declared to be "actual performance results"; they are, of course, unlikely to be "actual" for an activity that is as complex and difficult to observe as software development is. In practice, measurements will not be comprehensive, and inhabitants of the black box will gain control of the measurement instrument to make it report what will make them look good. In terms of the analogy, the thermometer reading will have little, if anything, to do with the real temperature. Problems with the control system will become apparent when something either burns up or freezes.

Despite problems with the analogy, it is not difficult to see how it might be attractive, especially to those technically trained and able to appreciate the elegance of the physical control model.[2] The attractiveness of mechanistic analogies derives in part from a human weakness for what Abraham Kaplan (1964) calls "the mystique of quantity," which he defines as "an exaggerated regard for the significance of measurement just because it is quantitative, without regard to what has been measured or to what can subsequently be done with the measure" (p. 172). For whatever reason, what is quantified often seems more attractive to some people than what is not quantified, even when what is quantified does not convey any more information. Max Singer

---

[2] Classical engineering control theory is a mathematically elegant field that involves differential equations, complex roots of polynomials, and clever graphical methods. Unfortunately for "organizational control theory" advocates, however, engineering control theory does not ordinarily assume self-interested behavior on the part of components of the control system.

(1971) writes of the vitality of mythical numbers, by which he means the tendency of a number, once produced, to take on a life of its own, to endure despite well-founded complaints about the method used to derive it. Richard O. Mason and E. Burton Swanson (1981, p. 398) observe that the claim by President John F. Kennedy that seventeen million Americans go to bed hungry every night was unsubstantiated and probably erroneous, but that it did help create social programs that now have budgets larger than those of most countries.

Failed redesigners of jobs mistakenly believe they have made the measurement system comprehensive. The different mistake made by those who believe in mechanistic analogies is their failure to understand that there are dire consequences of not accomplishing comprehensive measurements. The analogists tend to regard measurements as unbiased signals. The flaw in this conception, which is shared by agency theorists, has been discussed in previous chapters. The lack of understanding that leads to the mistake may derive from a well-documented human tendency to misunderstand conditional probability. A principal who believes with sound basis that favorable outcomes imply measurements in favorable ranges, may reason that therefore the reverse is true, that measurements in favorable ranges imply favorable outcomes. But the conclusion does not follow. Dawes (1988) discusses the human tendency to mistakenly assume that $p(A \mid B) = p(B \mid A)$; he points out how the mistake endures attempts to rectify it and how it has resulted in grievous consequences (such as when preventive mastectomies were based on erroneous estimates of cancer risk). As was noted in Chapter Two, Aristotle was likely the first to document this human failing, in *Poetics*, where he also described its persuasive power.

Even when dysfunction is discovered and it is revealed that full supervision has not been achieved, a principal may still resist the conclusion that full supervision cannot be achieved. She may conclude instead that she simply got it wrong when she attempted the last job redesign. An unending succession of attempts at job redesign may follow, as the principal tries earnestly to get it right. Some tasks may never yield to redesign. This pattern could be identified with current thinking about software development. There, as in many areas, the standardization reflex seems strong enough to obscure any alternative to measurement-based management. The result is that designers of software production systems are forever redesigning, replacing old modes of control, and substituting new but structurally similar modes, with predictable lack of success.

The Difficulty of the Principal's Inference Problem

Different control strategies implemented by the principal produce different outcomes. The outcomes are influenced both by random elements in nature and by effort allocations chosen by agents in response to the organizational control system. A stream of outcomes from an ongoing process like a software development project is not attributable to a single agent. Rather, the outcome stream is a noisy signal of the overall effectiveness of the control system. So, the principal faces an experiment: She can modify her control system and watch for changes in the outcome stream and in whatever she is measuring. She can repeat this indefinitely, and from repetition of this experiment, she should learn. She should acquire indications of whether she has successfully achieved full supervision.

Why the principal needs to experiment requires explanation. In terms of the model in the previous chapters, no experimentation is required. When the principal has perfect knowledge of the agent utility function, effort capacity, and costs of measurement—as assumed in previous chapters—then the model of motivational measurement tells her which mode of supervision to attempt and exactly where to locate targets. If knowledge of the measurement environment were perfect, there would be no problem in distinguishing full from partial supervision. But in real situations, the principal has perfect knowledge of very little. To gain knowledge she must experiment.

Lack of certain knowledge about the agent's effort capacity causes the principal to try to "feel it out," in what she believes are full supervision situations. Strategies for feeling out the effort capacity can manifest themselves as what could be called "naive continuous improvement." A common naive strategy involves starting targets at a level believed to be well within the agent's effort capacity, then incrementally moving the targets so that they become more challenging, until the agent's effort capacity is discovered. Other strategies involve encouraging agents to maximize on measured dimensions. A common way of encouraging agents to maximize is to put them in competition for rewards based on how they perform on measured dimensions. Increasing targets and competition between agents are both clearly parts of common management techniques like MBO and merit pay programs.[3]

Why is the inference problem so difficult for the principal? To see why requires revisiting Chapter Seven. Figure 7.3 has been reproduced here labeled as Fig. 14.1. Recall that under partial supervision, as targets are extended outward along the measurable dimension, the agent's effort allocation moves along the choice path, at first reaching higher same-value lines and improving value to the customer. In Fig. 14.1, movement from point B to point D increases value to the customer. Value improves less than it would under full supervision but, for a time, movement on the choice path and the expansion path are in roughly the same direction. Therefore, a principal who already believes that full supervision has been gained is likely to see a stream of outcomes that at first confirms her beliefs. In time, of course, it becomes apparent that full supervision has not been achieved. Points E and F are far from the best expansion path. By the time point F is reached, it should be clear from the outcome stream that there is something amiss.

---

[3] The situation being addressed here is more complicated than those depicted in the model in Chapters Four through Nine. That model was single-agent and static. Here, discussion has moved to multiple agents and repetition. What must be considered in this newly complex situation is whether introducing additional agents and repetition alters the way agents can be expected to react to targets. In some situations it might. However, casual experience reveals that people in real situations do try to meet targets set for them by their superiors in multi-agent settings. So, continuing by assuming that people do try to meet specified objectives is not very controversial.

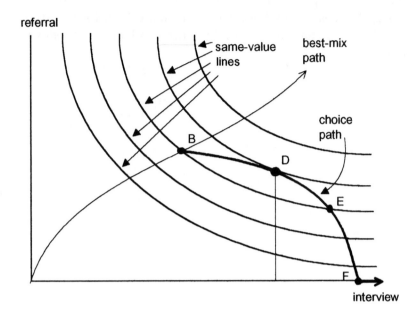

Figure 14.1: Why the principal's inference problem is difficult.

In some environments, however, outcomes are revealed very slowly. In software development, for example, evidence of a failed control system may only come to light after release of the software to customers, which could be years after the control system is introduced. When outcomes are revealed so slowly, learning is difficult. Because many things change between outcomes, it is not obvious how even consecutive outcomes should be compared. And even when evidence of a failed job redesign becomes impossible for designers to ignore, their reaction may be to attempt yet another redesign.

A principal might react to a failed control system by constructing another very similar system simply because she cannot imagine, and does not experience, the benefits of a significantly different alternative, such as delegatory management. Managing a measurement-based control system provides no experience relevant to alternative systems. A principal who learns experimentally will not gather data needed to compare delegatory and measurement-based alternatives, if she is not inclined to try the former. A principal is more likely to believe in the effectiveness of small changes in what she has been doing than in the effectiveness of large changes, especially since the latter will seem more risky.

Chapter Fifteen:
The Cynical Explanation of Dysfunction

The unimaginative principal might never consider alternatives to measurement-based control strategies and might not consider whether the task is at all suited to redesign for measurement. She might simply succumb to the standardization reflex, again and again. But it becomes increasingly difficult to believe in the earnest theory when principals repeatedly experience the cycle of job redesign, measurement, and dysfunction. Designers of measurement systems sometimes seem to continue in measurement-based control efforts despite knowing that their efforts are unlikely to work. This observation calls for a more "cynical" explanation of dysfunction in which system designers are assumed to exhibit guile.

The key fact to realize is that in a hierarchical organization every manager is an agent as well as a principal. Manager performance is very difficult to measure because of the intangible nature of managerial duties. There is substantial difficulty in determining how a firm or any of its components are doing. Even CEOs are agents, strictly speaking. And while a manager within a hierarchy might be responsible for design of a system of measurement and serve as principal to a set of agents, her own performance is judged mostly by how well her organization— that is, her agents—does according to the very measurement system the principal installs. The principal has an interest, then, in installing easily exploitable measurement systems. The hierarchical principal and agent quietly collude to their mutual benefit.

Likert (1961) argues that the tendency of organizations to rotate managers through assignments is a part of a strategy executed by organizational agents that allows them to make themselves look good. Managers set up rotational systems so that they will be able to take their positions knowing that the assignment's duration will be relatively short. At the beginning of the assignment, dysfunction appears due to the dysfunctional system put in place by the manager who just rotated out. The new manager puts in a new system that will show short-term results sure to impress—and which also will become dysfunctional after the manager rotates out, thereby giving yet another manager an opportunity to be impressive. There is no percentage in delegatory management for these managers, since delegation makes an impact primarily in the long term.

Even worse, failing to institute an exploitable measurement system can have severe costs. The lone agent who does what is good for the customer by refusing to meet dysfunctional targets not only loses any target-meeting bonuses but is also at risk for absorbing blame for the unfavorable outcomes caused, ironically, by the actions of everyone but him. This is a version of the dilemma described earlier that compels all agents to conform to dysfunctional incentive systems. If peer-group membership is at all fluid, then managers may also be prone to worry about a loose cannon who might come onto the scene and immediately begin behaving in a self-interested manner.

March (1984) discusses executive compensation in a similar light. He observes that "an intelligent manager learns that some of the more effective ways of improving profit and loss statements, or other indices of performance, have little to do with improving product, service, or technology," and that "it is often easier to manage the accounts of managerial or organizational performance than it is to manage the organization" (p. 57). March continues:

> By trying to manage accounts, executives try to convert outcomes that are difficult to control into out-

> comes over which they have some control. . . . If management involves a lottery with the potential for poor outcomes, a manager would like to be able to say, "I did the things a good manager should do." If one can claim to have done the things a good manager should do, bad outcomes can be seen as irrelevant to evaluation (pp. 57–58).

Account and reputation management are widespread because in many hierarchical organizations there is no true principal who conscientiously tries to achieve full supervision. As March notes, establishment of dysfunctional measurement systems is a risk aversion tactic for those who serve as surrogate principals within the hierarchy. When all managers meet their targets and are thus evaluated as performing well, the blame for failure can be cast on other causes, such as unfortunate events that might have occurred in the environment.

It is interesting to contemplate why there is no real principal in such an organization. The nesting of principals and agents in a hierarchy clearly provides incentives for collusion to produce measurements that can be subverted. What is puzzling is why the true principal, the owner of the organization's stream of production, does not insist on better measurement systems, or even no measurement system if no system is appropriate to the activities of the organization. Stockholders in a corporation surely want management to be effective—why do they not force this? One reason is that owners often have few tools at their disposal to influence the design or to force the abandonment of measurement systems. Their power to make changes is spread thinly and constrained by legal precedent that places primary responsibility for running a company with professional managers. Moreover, because they are not close to the activity of the organization, absentee owners are easily misled by the kinds of flawed analogies described under the "earnest explanation" heading in Chapter Fourteen. A situation that is probably common finds the owners of a firm, who are collectively the true principal, making earnest dysfunctional mistakes as their own hired managers actively lobby to reinforce mistaken impressions about the effectiveness of measurement.

It should not, of course, be concluded from this argument that all organizations are dominated by cynical behavior. What is being described here is how dysfunction happens and persists in organizations where it occurs. It does not always happen. Casual experience suggests that some organizations do better than others at avoiding dysfunction. Some organizations seem to have managers who are both earnest and shrewd. This observation leads to two compelling questions: 1) What is happening when organizations succeed at organizational control? and 2) Shouldn't organizations that are more successful at organizational control crowd out other, less successful organizations, in keeping with survival of the fittest?

Delegation Costs, Inevitable Dysfunction, and Non-Attributional Cultures

Opportunities for agents to engage in dysfunctional, self-interested behaviors are present in all organizations. So why do some organizations succeed at organizational control where others fail? The answer has to do with some of the same factors that were associated with low delegation costs in Chapter Eleven. Size, whether the organization is public or private, and the leadership abilities of executives are but a few of the factors already mentioned. Consistent with Dawes (1991), Ouchi (1981), Simon (1991), and some others, what is claimed here is that these factors are important to the extent that they influence feelings of group identification. These feelings cause people who share membership in an organization or other group to forego acts of covert opportunism, like designing easily corruptible measurement systems that would be to their individual benefit but to the group's detriment.

Measurement looks even less attractive as a means of control when considered in light of this conclusion. Managers are less likely to behave with dysfunctional guile when they feel a sense of group identity. But when there is widely felt group identity within the organization, the costs of delegation tend to be low also; delegatory management, with its structural advantages over control by measurement (as shown in Chapter Eleven), can more easily be achieved in these organizations. In other words, when managers are likely to be earnest, delegation is relatively more attractive anyway. Also, as E.L. Deci and R.M. Ryan (1985) and many others have shown, internal motivation deteriorates in the presence of external incentives. Feelings of group identity and allegiance to the firm are degraded by the institution of measurements; the very act of installing a measurement system makes it more likely that managers will behave with guile. The lack of trust implied when managers see that they are being measured makes them more likely to distrust those who are doing the measuring; managers are therefore inclined to design safeguards for themselves (that is, potential avenues of subversion) into the system, to the extent that they are able to influence design (and usually they are). In this sense, measurement systems often undermine themselves.

Although it seems obvious, it is important to emphasize that individuals do not always react in a self-interested way when exposed to dysfunctional temptations, whether in organizations or in other social settings. To borrow from an example from DeMarco's interview, Weimar Republic Jews revealed their true religion to census-takers despite their well-established history of persecution. Software developers in Tilford's red-pen example were very trusting before the executive with the red pen came on the scene. As Dawes (1991) relates, people tend to put aside their individual interests in favor of group interests. It has been shown (in Chapter Eleven) that organizations that succeed in creating group identity and using delegation to control organizational activity have certain structural advantages over those that do not. This suggests that there should be some learning and natural selection taking place at the group level. Rationality may be operating, imperfectly, at the group level rather than the individual level. If so, organizations that are successful at control should be crowding out organizations that are unsuccessful.

Whether organizations are moving more toward delegation is extremely difficult to test. It is possible to make a case that organizations are moving away from measurement-based control strategies. But any movement toward delegation is certainly halting, and it must be admitted that there is counter-evidence. For example, Chapter Three pointed out that Western firms seem increasingly to be tying compensation to measures of performance. Nevertheless, many recent trends in management have tended in the direction of delegation. The ideas of the Human Relations School have been remarkably resilient since the 1950s, although the names used to describe many ideas have changed. Empowerment and participative management, which are currently popular, are based on ideas first espoused under the rubric of human relations.

Ouchi (1981) offers considerable anecdotal evidence to suggest that Japanese firms have attained world-class performance because they are better at delegation than many Western firms. Table 15.1 is borrowed from Ouchi (1981, p. 58) and shows how Japanese and American organizations compare on a number of managerial tendencies. It is not difficult to see that Japanese methods are more consistent with nurturing group identity while American methods tend to emphasize competition between agents.

Table 15.1.
Cross-Cultural Control Comparisons (Ouchi, 1981).

Japanese Organizations	American Organizations
Lifetime Employment	Short-term Employment
Slow Evaluation and Promotion	Rapid Evaluation and Promotion
Non-specialized Career Paths	Specialized Career Paths
Implicit Control Mechanisms	Explicit Control Mechanisms
Collective Decision Making	Individual Decision Making
Collective Responsibility	Individual Responsibility
Wholistic Concern	Segmented Concern

Two anecdotes from Ouchi (1981) further emphasize the degree to which Japanese firms rely on delegation, in contrast with more measurement-based American methods. In the first, the Japanese president of the American subsidiary of a Japanese bank refuses to give his American managers the performance targets for which they are begging. The Japanese bank president's reasons are revealing:

> If only I could get these Americans to understand our philosophy of banking. To understand what the business means to us—how we feel we should deal with our customers and our employees. What our relationship should be to the local communities we serve. How we should deal with our competitors, and what our role should be in the world at large. If they could get that under their skin, then they could figure out for themselves what an appropriate objective would be for any situation, no matter how unusual or new, and I would never have to tell them, never have to give them a target (pp. 40–41).

The managers in this example, all trained in the American tradition, seem to see no advantage in setting objectives unless measures will later show their president how managers have performed. In contrast, the president does not care how well they perform with respect to any measures he might create but instead prefers that they do what is necessary, creating objectives and measures for themselves if that is helpful to them.

The second anecdote is an account of an American electronics company's management of a new factory built in Japan. The company, widely considered to be among the most creative of American firms, decided to make a thorough study of Japanese workers and design a factory that combined the best features of Eastern and Western factories. The company discovered that Japanese firms almost never use individual incentive schemes, like piece-work systems, or even individual performance appraisals applied to salary increases. Company officials reasoned that rewarding individual achievement was one of the best features of Western management and so planned a piece-work compensation system for use on the factory floor. When the plant was built, Japanese women wired together an electronics product under an incentive system that awarded each woman payment proportional to the average speed at which she worked. Two months after the plant opened, the supervisors approached the plant manager, saying,

> . . . we are embarrassed to be so forward, but we must speak to you because all of the girls have threatened to quit work this Friday. Why can't our plant have the same compensation system as other Japanese companies? When you hire a new girl, her starting wage should be fixed by her age. An eighteen-year-old should be paid more than a sixteen-year-old. Every year on her birthday, she should receive an automatic increase in pay. The idea that any one of us can be more productive than another must be wrong, because none of us in final assembly could make a thing unless all of the other people in the plant had done their jobs right first. To single one person out as being more productive is wrong and is also personally humiliating to us (p. 48).

The plant changed its compensation policy. Deming (1986), Larkey and Caulkins (1992), and perhaps a few others argue insightfully that individual incentive systems are just as problematic in Western as in Eastern manifestations. The anecdote provides insight into Deming's claim (Gabor, 1989) that performance measurement is one of Western management's most misguided policies.

Dawes and J.M. Orbell (1992) suggest that people who tend to forego individual interests in dilemma situations might successfully form groups through use of simple heuristics. Resulting groups are more capable of internal selfless cooperation and compete well against organizations composed of people who are not prone to cooperate. In a similar manner, organizations might be able to nurture group identity by choosing members who are more prone toward such feelings. This may be what a company's recruiters mean when they say they are looking for "team players." Organizations often overtly seek cooperativeness in prospective employees. Rohlen (1974), in his study of a Japanese bank, documents the exhaustive lengths to which some companies in Japan go to make sure that a prospective employee is compatible with the company's culture. He describes the bank's rather extreme efforts to investigate the families, religions, and personal lives of job candidates. Efforts of this sort would be illegal in many Western nations, but the point remains relevant: An organization's efforts to align the interests of its members through delegatory means can be aided by careful attempts to select cooperators as members.

What comes through in the anecdotes is a picture of a form of organizational control that can be referred to as a *non-attributional culture*. In the non-attributional culture, systems of measurement do not motivate employees who fear for their career prospects and future rewards. Attribution and blame is unthinkable within the culture. Motivation is derived from wanting the group to succeed. Measurements are a means of obtaining information and their limitations are widely acknowledged. Measurements are not the central obsession of managers, nor are they the main tool for managing. They are, in fact, beside the point somewhat, secondary to discovery of information through walking around and talking to people doing the work about what the real problems are. In the non-attributional culture, people are inclined—as is urged in a Japanese proverb—to fix the problem, not the blame. This organizational climate adjusts the preferences of workers so that aversion to effort is minimized and desire to help the group by doing well for the customer is maximized.

Organizations do not easily attain this ideal, nor do they easily maintain it once it is achieved (recall the red-pen example—things were going along fine until the red pen came on the scene). Consider Table 15.1 again. It is not difficult to predict what would happen in American firms that abruptly began to behave as Japanese firms do. If a company announced a policy of slow evaluation and promotion, employees would leave that firm in droves. Employees might similarly balk at a removal of performance evaluation systems that they can control and that thus help them avert risk. Because of historical and cultural factors, Western firms might only be able to move in a delegatory direction through use of a sound transition strategy. A transition strategy would probably heavily emphasize procedural safeguards against measurement abuse. After some period in which procedural safeguards were in place, perhaps the culture would have changed enough to expand the uses of measurement and realize all of its informational benefits. In such a culture, fear would be thoroughly driven out (Deming, 1986).

There is reason for optimism. Dawes's results are a reminder that people can be induced into cooperation with relative ease in certain situations. Employees in the red-pen story were eagerly participating in the measurement program before the arrival of the loose-cannon president. People seem to have a deep-rooted desire to trust, cooperate, and participate in many real settings.

Chapter Sixteen:

Interviews with Software Measurement Experts

I nterviews conducted with renowned experts reveal what is considered to be state-of-the-art thinking about the use of measurement in software development. Computer software development is an intriguing case for two reasons. First, interest in measurement is high among software practitioners, so the issues raised here are relevant to practice. Second, the model developed here suggests that software development is usually poorly suited to measurement-based control. There is reason to believe, then, that this production activity might provide opportunities to study dysfunction.

The interviews consisted of 26 open-ended questions about organizational measurement organized into six sections. Sections 1 through 5 were designed to elicit expert answers to the following overall questions:

1. *What is the purpose of organizational measurement and what are the advantages and disadvantages of using it?*

2. *What uses of measurement are appropriate and productive and what uses are inappropriate or counterproductive?*

3. *Is there a conflict between uses of measurement (for example, between motivational and informational uses) and, if so, how serious is the conflict?*

4. *Is it possible to develop a system of measurement for software development that cannot be undermined (that is, can full supervision of software development be achieved), and if so, how hard is it to implement such a system?*

5. *What causes measurement dysfunction and how serious a problem is it?*

Section 6 of the interview presented the experts with several statements, some seemingly innocuous, others potentially controversial (for example, "Metrics provide managers with a way of identifying employees who are especially strong or weak performers"), and asked experts to discuss their degree of agreement or disagreement with the statement. A detailed description of questions and interview methods can be found in the Appendix.

For each of the 26 interview questions, the model developed in earlier chapters generates an unambiguous answer that can be compared to experts' answers. Interviews were recorded and transcribed, then analyzed and scored for agreement with this book's model. Two points were scored for solid agreement, one point for partial agreement, and no points for disagreement. In addition, answers to five summary questions, called "X-Questions," were derived from the overall content of each expert interview. The X-Questions address details of organizational measurement situations that are considered key in the context of this book's model. The X-Questions were scored by the same method used for the 26 interview questions, but their totals have been kept separate. In the discussions that follow, scores associated with the five summary questions are referred to as X-Scores.

Complete agreement with the model constructed in this book results in a score of 52 on the interview questions and 10 on the X-Questions. Complete disagreement with the model translates into scores of 0 for both sets of questions.

Interview Results

Table 16.1 summarizes overall results from scoring the eight interviews, along with some expert attributes. Total Scores range from a low of 20 to a high of nearly perfect agreement at 51. X-Scores range from 0 to nearly perfect agreement at 9. The experts' scores cluster interestingly. Experts 6, 7, and 8 are in good agreement with the model. There is one, Expert 3, in the middle range at a total score of 34, and the rest cluster in the low to mid 20s. This observation suggests an analysis to determine whether the group clustered in the 20s had similar beliefs. If so, perhaps they are advocates of a different model. Alternatively, common elements in answers by experts who are not in agreement with the model presented in this book may be evidence of the systematic errors described in the explanation of dysfunction.

Table 16.1.
Total Scores and X-Scores.

	SEI Affiliated?	Publications	Industry or Consultant	Self-estimate of Metrics Systems Encountered	Total Scores	X-Scores
Expert 1	Yes	Extensive	I	30	22	0
Expert 2	Yes	Some	C	20 to 40	20	0
Expert 3	Yes	Extensive	I	10 to 15	34	6
Expert 4	No	Extensive	C	Hundreds	25	0
Expert 5	Yes	Extensive	C	Low Thousands	26	0
Expert 6	Yes	Extensive	I	Thousands	38	7
Expert 7	No	Some	I	Hundreds	42	7
Expert 8	No	Extensive	C	80 to 90	51	9

Table 16.2.
Raw Scores.

Question Number	Exp. 1 (22)	Exp. 2 (20)	Exp. 3 (34)	Exp. 4 (25)	Exp. 5 (26)	Exp. 6 (38)	Exp. 7 (42)	Exp. 8 (51)	Question Total
1	1	1	1	2	2	2	2	2	13
2	1	1	2	2	2	2	2	2	14
3	0	2	2	0	2	0	2	2	10
4	1	1	1	1	1	2	2	2	11
5	1	1	2	2	1	2	2	2	13
6	0	0	1	1	2	2	2	2	10
7	1	0	1	0	0	1	2	2	7
8	2	1	2	0	1	2	2	2	12
9	0	1	2	2	2	2	2	2	13
10	0	0	0	0	0	2	2	2	6
11	2	2	2	1	2	2	2	2	15
12	0	0	2	2	0	1	1	2	8
13	1	0	2	1	1	1	2	2	10
14	0	1	1	2	2	2	2	2	12
15	2	1	0	0	2	2	2	2	11
16	2	2	1	1	0	0	1	2	9
17	1	1	0	1	1	1	0	2	7
18	2	2	1	1	0	2	1	2	11
19	2	2	2	2	1	2	2	2	15
20	2	0	2	2	2	2	2	2	14
21	1	1	1	2	2	1	2	2	12
X1	0	0	0	0	0	2	0	1	3
X2	0	0	2	0	0	2	2	2	8
X3	0	0	0	0	0	0	1	2	3
X4	0	0	2	0	0	2	2	2	8
X5	0	0	2	0	0	1	2	2	7

Table 16.2 shows how each expert scored on every question. The last column shows the total for each question across all experts. When all experts are in perfect agreement with the model, the last column contains a 16; total disagreement with the model is shown by 0 in the last column. By looking at questions with high and low numbers in the total column, it is possible to get a sense of the experts' points of general agreement and disagreement with the model. Consider scores of 14 or higher to indicate relatively uniform agreement among experts with the model, and scores below 10 to represent general disagreement. Highlighting questions in this way produces a startling pattern.

First, consider points of agreement. Almost all experts strongly agreed that the primary reason to measure in software development was informational rather than motivational. This can be seen from question 2, which asked about advantages of using measurement; every expert responded by emphasizing informational uses of measurement. Also, the agreement illustrated by question 20, which asked if measurement could provide a way of identifying strong and weak employee performance, as well as the emphatic tone used in responses to this question (the phrase "absolutely not!" came up a lot here), indicates a strong consensus on the primary purpose of measurement in software settings. The other point of conspicuous agreement was that there is potential for measurement problems when measurements are used to evaluate agents; agreement here is evidenced by question 11, which asked about employee reactions to being measured, and question 20. So, interestingly, it seems that all experts agree with the model on two fundamental points. They want measurement to be primarily informational and not motivational; and they are aware of the potential for dysfunction.

Disagreements reveal themselves at the next level of detail, in a premise about the measurement context. Question 10, which asked whether it is possible to construct comprehensive measures in software development, is extremely revealing. It shows that all experts other than the three in good agreement with the model believe that it is possible for software measurement systems to be comprehensive. This is consistent with the dysfunctional mistake referred to in Chapter Fourteen. Experts 1 through 5 believe that full supervision often occurs in the context of software measurement. That this is true comes out also in their responses.

To the follow-up question, "You feel in your organization there's not that great of an opportunity to play with the numbers?" Expert 3 responded by saying, "In fact, especially in software development [because of our extensive measurement system]." Expert 2 said unequivocally, "Can [measurements] be so robust that people can't tamper with them?—Yes."

Because they believe that full supervision can be achieved, these experts believe valuable incentives can be provided to agents, which is consistent with their answers to questions 16, 17, and X2, all of which address linking incentive schemes and measurement systems. Since they believe full supervision often occurs, they also see no necessary incompatibility between motivational uses of measurement and informational uses (question 7). Also, as a consequence of their belief in full supervision, disagreeing experts are not as concerned about air-tight precautions against motivational measurement (questions 12, X1, X5), do not consider the danger of measurement gone awry as serious (X3), and see no necessary danger in giving measurement information to management (X4). The point of great interest here is that *all points of significant disagreement are consistent with the classic dysfunctional error of assuming full supervision when it cannot occur.* This suggests the validity of the explanation of dysfunction offered in this book.

One wonders, however, given that they believe that full supervision often occurs, why the experts who disagree with the model on question 10 (about feasibility of comprehensive measurement) worry about dysfunction at all. To the extent that they do worry about it, one wonders how they think it arises. One reason why they seem to worry about dysfunction is that they have observed it. However, these "disagreers" interpret dysfunction differently from those whose answers are more consistent with the model. Where "agreers" regard dysfunction as a consequence of the structure of incentives in a situation, disagreers seem to think of dysfunction as a response induced by indelicate supervisory styles of individual managers. For example, Expert 1, when asked if metrics should be used to motivate, responds "Yes, but very, very carefully—it's a lot easier to use them to de-motivate employees." Expert 2's discussion of the use of measurement in employee performance review is in a similar spirit:

> I'm saying that even with respect to your performance reviews, there's a set of objectives that you're working to quantify. . . . it's a part of my performance reviews. I go in with quantitative information. Let's say that I'm reviewing [colleague name]. He comes in; he sits down. And, I've collected all of this information, and I say, "You know all of your modules have had all of these defects associated with them. What the hell is going on?" All of a sudden I've tied it so much to him that it's no longer a catalyst for improvement. But, if I come in and say, "You know, through the years, as you know, we've been collecting this information, and it looks like what we need to work on for the next year is human-computer interface issues; you need to really improve the way you do your work in this area because it looks like you've had a lot of defects associated with that area, and maybe what you need to do is sign up for some courses, improve your knowledge in this area, and then try to work in a team." If I say it that way, you're more inclined to look at this and say, "Yeah, you know what, there is some information and I really better look at improving a specific area," versus, "Oh, my god, I just got fifty demerits, and I'm not going to get . . . "

Sometimes some experts appear to contradict themselves. Expert 5 provides a dramatic example of a kind of turn-about that allows one to worry and also to not worry about dysfunction. After arguing eloquently that measurements should not be done in an evaluative manner because of the potential for dysfunction, he offers an idea:

> You can even incentivize it in terms of, you know, bonuses and goals that are realistic that they might earn some extra money from. [*Unscripted interviewer follow-up: What sort of incentives are you talking about*

> *there?*] They can be incentives like monetary incentives for reaching a milestone on time, getting the job done, meeting a certain quality standard, delivering a product that, you know, has a Mean Time to Failure of two days at the time it's delivered—in other words, it runs in its operating environment, does what it's supposed to do for at least two days without any defects. So, those are things that can be measured, demonstrated, and can be rewarded with bonuses to the project team, and they'll all feel kind of good about that.

This expert is careful to emphasize that rewards should be given to the group, not individuals, but he never addresses the accidental association of rewards with, say, project managers, or the ability of groups to collude to subvert measurements. In contrast, Expert 6 (who is in agreement with the model) brings the matter up immediately on being asked whether metrics should report status on projects (question 4):

> My feeling with software metrics is that when you have something being measured that is potentially identifiable to the person so that it might affect that person's performance rating—if it's that kind of measurement—then only that engineer or manager should get data about his or her own performance, OK? Then it's reasonable to give them data on the statistics, that is, the average and, say, the standard deviation of comparable projects. For example, if I were a project manager, and data were being collected on, say, the number of faults found in the code, I would not be able to see that individual data. Each person would be able to see his or her own data and the statistics so they could compare themselves against somebody else. But I would get only the average. I would get the data from my project, and I would get data on the averages of the projects of other project managers. But I wouldn't see Tom Smith's, for example. I wouldn't see how his project is doing.

This expert is concerned about an unintended effect of the measurement system. The three experts who agreed most closely with the model shared this high level of concern for unintended effects. They were concerned not only about what a measurement system would be on installation, but also what it would become over time. Experts who disagreed showed sporadic concern for factors that might convert measurement systems into something unintended; for example, Expert 1 observed that "you cannot control what managers do—it's almost like a matter of time before the head guy's saying, 'Well, who did the good job here and who did the bad job?'" But Experts 6, 7, and 8 (especially 7 and 8) were unusual for their continued high level of concern about unintended effects, and also in their willingness to include costs due to the risk of a measurement program going out of control in their evaluation of the worth of the measurement concept. These three experts were more likely than others to speak of measurement systems as having costs and to accept the notion that a program of measurement must justify itself.

Expert 7's discussion of individual productivity measures fits nearly perfectly with the model:

> . . . let's say we have some individual productivity kind of measurement. . . . even if you could do it, I don't think it's a good idea. I think it's the best way in the world to kill your measurement program. I've seen it backfire so badly when people try to personalize it, and I also believe it's very difficult to measure productivity, to be perfectly honest with you . . . [*Unscripted interviewer follow-up: So when it backfires, do people rebel against it, or do they*—] Yeah, in a subtle kind of way. It's not like they campaign against it openly. They just very subtly—sort of, kind of benign neglect.

The same expert's views on performance evaluation systems reads like an argument for delegatory management of software development that might have come right out of the model:

> It's natural for me to assume that when someone comes to work, they really want to do the job, . . . but

things get in their way. . . . I don't think I have honestly ever met someone who came to work on a given day intentionally setting out to screw the place up—OK? So, I wonder, What is the value of this process that causes so much agony? I also was very frustrated with the process of personally evaluating people because inevitably it seemed like I would get caught in a situation where there was an expectation, with people above me, that a certain distribution should occur in the performance of the organization. Especially when I had larger organizations, they expected a certain kind of a curve, kind of a distribution where a certain percentage of them would be at the top, and a larger percentage lower down, and so forth. And it was always funny to me because when we hired people, [we] always hired the best—OK? Now the best came in, and a year later, we evaluated them, and suddenly they weren't the best anymore. And I always wondered, "What did we do to them?" The whole thing just bothers my sense of logic. It didn't seem that it ever really added to the potential of the organization. . . . when people in the organization felt that they were respected and they had value, and that they could make mistakes and that was OK, and that we all do, they just seemed to start having more successes. So, I have never seen [performance measurement] as a very good thing.

Expert 8 verbalized intuitions that correspond to very subtle points in the model. Early in his interview, he confronted foundational issues having to do with measurement in organizations. When asked if he considered himself an advocate of software metrics, he spoke in the following way of costs and risks associated with measurement systems:

Well, do you mean advocating—as opposed to not measuring—things? Well, yes. It doesn't follow from that that more measurement is better and most best. I think it's very important. I mean measurement is enormously expensive, and is a technique which suffers from a terrible tendency toward institutionalization.

Later, he had more to say on the dangers of institutionalization of measurement systems:

> I will say . . . against the metrics programs . . . the ones that want to institutionalize metrics too much, that didn't have a judicious hand in applying metrics . . . [they] ended up being way too expensive and too top heavy and boring. . . . The people were on call too much of the time to collect data about themselves. It interfered with their doing what they really wanted to do.

In a similar vein, describing a program he considered a failure, Expert 8 said:

> They built far too much of the measurement into the process. The process was measuring itself at all points, and they lost track of their underlying goals. . . . They measured forever and ever. . . .

His diagnosis in this case is interesting because it is common among measurement experts to advocate arrangements in which development programs have extensively built-in measurement capabilities. In contrast, Expert 8 regards this as a recipe for losing sight of ends in the pursuit of the means. He also expressed willingness to consider whether the dysfunctional effects of measurement might follow inevitably when measurement is used in organizational contexts.

Expert 8 was alone among interviewed experts in suggesting that his beliefs concerning measurement had evolved over time. He describes the transition in his beliefs from the time when he published his first book on the subject of measurement in software development up until the present in a way that sounds consistent with moving from the dysfunctional mistake toward thinking in accord with the model:

I think my book seemed to make the point that metrics are so good, that there's just no limit to how many we'd like to have, and I was very naive, I think. Metrics are terribly expensive and it would be a disastrous error to institute use of a metric forever-after when, in fact, it's value was entirely on a one-time basis.

Results from the expert interviews also support an important part of the explanation of dysfunction put forward in Chapter Fifteen. That chapter argued that dysfunctional measurement systems persist because managers and consultants have a vested interest in maintaining easy-to-control measurement systems so that they can look good to their superiors and clients. An extension of that argument suggests that consultants, who are less likely to identify with an organization than the organization's own managers, might be more inclined to harbor beliefs consistent with a dysfunctional pattern.

In the interviews, the four industry experts averaged 34.0 and 5.0, on Total- and X-Scores, respectively. The numbers for consultants were 30.5 and 2.25. If Expert 8 is removed from the group of consultants, the rest are not at all in agreement with the model; their Total-Score average is 23.7 and their X-Score average is 0. Consultants, who are not a part of an organization and thus do not identify with it and who stand to benefit greatly from guile and convenient beliefs, are ready prey to dysfunctional pressures.

Chapter Seventeen:

The Measurement Disease

![black bar separator]

The model presented in this book implies that many leading-edge management methods are inappropriate for their organizational contexts. For many such methods, it is not difficult to find examples of mistaken analogies and of individuals profiting from perpetuation of flawed notions and methods. Three popular but flawed methods are examined in this chapter. Analysis of the three methods in the context of the model reveals how dramatically counter to conventional management wisdom recommendations derived from the model can be and how different are this book's explanation of why these methods are so popular. The three methods are the Malcolm Baldrige National Quality Award, the ISO 9000 certification process, and the Software Engineering Institute's (SEI) Software Capability Evaluation (SCE).

The Malcolm Baldrige Quality Award

On April 20, 1987, then-President Ronald Reagan signed the Malcolm Baldrige National Quality Improvement Act, which called for creation of a national award and the development of guidelines that organizations could use to evaluate their quality improvement efforts (Garvin, 1991). The Act mentioned several management principles and tools, but gave no guidance on the

Award's scoring system or judging process. The National Institute of Standards and Technology was commissioned to fill in the details. The result was a seven-category, thousand-point scoring system and a three-level judging process. Companies who want to compete submit a 50- to 75-page application, which is "graded" by a group of industry quality experts. High scorers earn site visits. Examiners visit these companies, interviewing and checking claims made on applications. After the site visits, judges pick winners. Winners were first selected in 1988.

Applicants for the Award must show evidence of excellence in their business practices in seven areas: leadership, information and analysis, strategic quality planning, human resource development, management of process quality, operational results, and customer focus. Materials provided with applications and a substantial and growing literature provide information on what constitutes evidence of success in these areas. Consultants stand ready to provide organizations with help in preparing their applications and site visit presentations. Roughly 75 percent of points awarded are allocated to process criteria, leaving only about 25 percent of the scoring on product quality.

Winners of the Baldrige Award experience a windfall of favorable publicity. Some past winners have been able to generate revenues from their Baldrige experience by providing consulting services to firms still trying to win. More significant than the additional revenues is the prestige associated with winning. Winning a Baldrige is one way for a management team to show stockholders that they are doing a good job. Managers' incentives to win can be considerable.

ISO 9000 Certification

ISO 9000 is a series of five quality standards (numbered from 9000 to 9004) set by the International Standards Organization (ISO). Organizations are assessed by third parties to determine whether their business practices meet one of the standards; an organization that meets the standard appropriate to its type of business can legally advertise its "ISO 9000 certification." Certification is increasingly important for companies that trade internationally. All firms that trade within the European

Common Market are legally required to be ISO 9000 certified; the standards have been adopted in greater or lesser degree by 35 countries around the world (Marquardt, 1992). Even in countries where certification is not mandated, customers are increasingly asking whether prospective suppliers are certified. The purpose of the ISO 9000 series of standards is to provide a means by which customers can be assured that suppliers are using quality business practices without having to perform individual audits of each prospective supplier.

The ISO 9000 standards establish requirements for the systems of production within the facilities of a company. They are not product standards, but rather *process* standards, which require that certain process characteristics are in place. For example, one standard (ISO 9002) contains stipulations such as "those processes affecting quality must be monitored and controlled" and "objective evidence must be provided that the product received and delivered is inspected or otherwise verified" (Gasko, 1992, p. 18). The standard approach to achieving ISO 9000 certification involves comprehensively documenting all processes involved in production and in support of production. In the course of documenting, processes are reviewed and evaluated to determine if they are up to the standard. Where they are not, corrective action is taken. The goal is to create a situation in which "you document what you do, and do what you document" (Marquardt, 1992, p. 51). Successfully achieving this situation will result in certification. Usually, informal self-assessments are performed at various stages on the way to certification, to determine the likely outcome of a formal assessment. When results of self-assessments are satisfactory, the organization employs a third party to conduct a certification assessment.

The ISO 9000 series of standards was written by a committee of the ISO composed of delegates from the international community.[1] Delegates composed the standards by combining aspects of

---

[1] Unlike in the West, there has been an absence of enthusiasm in Japan for registration of quality systems by third-party certification bodies (McFadyen and Walsh, 1992). However, the Japanese have become considerably more interested in the ISO 9000 standards since it became clear that they would need to be certified to maintain access to their markets.

military standards, nuclear power plant regulations, medical device regulations, and other regulations and standards from delegate countries. ISO 9000 is widely deployed in the European Union (EU), as well as in countries with close ties to the EU (for example, New Zealand). Manufacturers in the U.S., such as DuPont, Union Carbide, and a variety of others who trade in significant volume with EU clients, are busily certifying their facilities to maintain access to their markets. Because firms literally will be barred from their markets if they are not certified, the incentive to achieve certification is substantial.

Software Capability Evaluation

A Software Capability Evaluation is an assessment of an organization's process for developing software as it relates to a particular parcel of work for which the U.S. government plans to contract (SEI, 1991). It is a tool intended to help a government agency determine the organization's ability to produce a particular product on time, within budget, and with high quality. The evaluation is conducted by trained government auditors. Because the SEI's efforts are government-sponsored, the program is being widely deployed across government agencies. Consequently, businesses that do contract work for the government are taking interest.

An SCE evaluates the process used by the contractor to develop software to see how well it conforms to ideals expressed in the Capability Maturity Model (CMM). The CMM is a distillation of what SEI scientists, based on their research and experience, believe to be an ideal form of software development. It is based on quality assurance principles promulgated by Philip Crosby (1979). SCEs make use of a standard questionnaire and follow-up interviews to determine key process areas in which an organization shows weakness, as well as the organization's maturity level. A maturity level is a number, 1 through 5, with 1 lowest and 5 highest, which summarizes the organization's excellence in software development process. A standard scoring algorithm is used to arrive at the maturity level. There is limited empirical data that shows a correlation between evaluated maturity levels and quality in software product or effectiveness of development process as determined by some external measure. Meanwhile, consultants stand ready to provide organizations with advice on what has caused other firms to "pass" their SCEs.

It is generally assumed among government contractors that it is only a matter of time before all organizations that provide software to government agencies will be required to achieve a certain level of maturity. There have been suggestions that maturity level 3 is the aspiration of Department of Defense officials, and it is expected that other agencies will follow suit, perhaps as required by an Act of Congress. Such suggestions are of considerable concern to contractors since only 7 percent of organizations were at level 3 as reported in a comprehensive study of SCEs in 1991. None were at level 4 or 5. Many of these contractors do a very large percentage of their business with the U.S. government. Continued access to the better portion of their revenues depends (or is expected to depend), then, on favorable outcomes of SCEs.

Similarities Between Methods

Certain similarities in the above methods should already be apparent. First, each of the methods consists of an audit, performed by an external examiner who intends to find fault in the firm's business practices. Second, the models used for comparison with a firm's practices are primarily oriented toward measuring characteristics of business processes rather than products (that is, interim rather than end results). Third, there is a standard instrument used to determine the scoring of evaluations, and the nature of the instrument is intentionally made known to the firms that will be audited.[2] Fourth, what each instrument attempts to evaluate is a very complex set of practices across sometimes very large firms. And fifth, in each case, the firm has tremendous incentive to achieve favorable evaluation.

Each of these evaluation methods constitutes a sort of measurement-based control system, with potential for dysfunction. A firm's business practices provide value to a customer because of

---

[2] For example: "A further objective [of SCEs] is to provide a public process which is defined in advance and for which the contractors can prepare" (Humphrey and Sweet, 1987).

effort allocations across a very great number of effort dimensions. The instruments associated with these programs may perform measurements on many effort dimensions, but it is unlikely, bordering on impossible, that the standard instruments cover all of the customer's critical dimensions. Full supervision is not likely here because of the large number of activities critical to customer value, and because it is likely that there are disparities in the cost of measuring across dimensions. And, it is an explicit part of each of these programs that incentives are sufficient to induce agents to meet the targets embedded in the standard instruments.

One feature of these programs that might seem to be an advantage over many systems of measurement—even a saving grace—is that the programs here rely on point-in-time rather than continuous measurements. Recall that in real situations, agents only gradually learn to exploit the measurement system. Administering measurement only one time might forestall agents' learning about and exploiting the system. Valid information might consequently be provided by such a system. Consistent with this notion, Garvin (1991), a defender of the Baldrige Award, claims that "it provides companies with a comprehensive framework for assessing their progress toward the new paradigm of management and such commonly acknowledged goals as customer satisfaction and increased employee involvement" (p. 80).

Such contentions begin to seem problematic, however, when one considers some of the behavior of firms in and around these management methods. Firms seem to work very hard to learn how to exploit the program measures *before* they are administered. For example, there have been reports of enormous investments by companies in preparation for examiners' visits. Xerox, a winner, and Corning, a finalist, have confessed spending respectively $800,000 and 14,000 labor hours preparing applications and instructing employees on how to behave during examiners' site visits (Garvin, 1991). Another very significant problem with the Baldrige Award is that examiners are also consultants, which creates potential for conflicts of interest (Crosby, 1992). ISO 9000 also has this problem (Fouhy *et al.*, 1992). Consequently, many of the same people who provide advice on how to win the Baldrige or how to achieve ISO certification may later perform audits on their own clients. Companies who want audits to go well can enter into a cozy relationship with a consultant/auditor. The chairman of one quality consulting firm confides that "currently 80–90 percent of the companies going through the [ISO] certification are just wasting their money" if their intention is truly to improve quality (Fouhy *et al.*, 1992, p. 45).

Sometimes, evidence that firms have ramped up to corrupt a one-time audit appears in the firm's behavior after the audit. In attempting to become the first U.S. company to win the Japanese equivalent of the Baldrige Award, called the Deming Award, Florida Power and Light Company (FP&L) seems to have expended a great deal of its resources. Interestingly, though, the resources were redirected after the award was won:

> In the late 1980s, [FP&L] acquired all the trappings of an extensive quality programme in its bid to become the first non-Japanese winner of the Deming prize—an 85-strong quality department, 1,900 quality teams involving three quarters of its employees, and a rigorous, highly statistical, "quality-review" system. FP&L won its Deming prize in 1989. But while customers saw some improvements in the quality of its services, these were insignificant when set against the sheer scale of the firm's quality effort. To a large extent, FP&L was just going through the motions. One utilities regulator, visiting an FP&L nuclear power station, noted that many employees seemed as interested in the appearance of quality as in quality itself. . . . FP&L's head of quality is clearing up the mess. The quality department now has only six employees; most of the quality teams have been disbanded; the whole process is "a lot less rigid" ("The Cracks in the Quality," *The Economist,* April 18, 1992, p. 67).

The debriefing teams that have been rumored to appear in firms subject to SCEs are an example of revealing *during*-audit behavior. Debriefing teams interview members of a firm immediately following their interactions with SCE evaluators, attempting to find out what was said in the interviews. One effect, surely intended, is to intimidate employees who might be inclined to say unflattering things about the firm. Debriefing teams have been rumored to launch clandestine investigations to determine which firm members made damaging remarks that cost the organization in its rating.

Further evidence of corruption of such audits might be found in the lack of correlation between audit results and other measures of firm performance. It has been noted by many that Baldrige winners do not have systematically better quality than their competitors (Garvin, 1991). Nor do Baldrige winners necessarily experience better sales and earnings growth than their peers. Cadillac, Motorola, IBM, and Federal Express are all said to have suffered major marketplace setbacks since winning the Baldrige. Symptoms of dysfunctional manipulation can be found even in what is often offered as evidence of the Award's effectiveness. The General Accounting Office (GAO, 1990) studied twenty Baldrige winners and high scorers to determine whether they exhibited better overall performance than peer firms. The GAO determined that there was a cause-and-effect relationship between Total Quality Management practices embodied in the Baldrige criteria and corporate performance as measured by employee relations, productivity, customer satisfaction, or profitability. However, the study was "not performed scientifically using statistical methods, and the twenty participating companies did not answer all questions" (Garvin, 1991, p. 84). In fact, the average rate of response on each question was only nine of twenty firms. The low response rate can easily be interpreted as yet another example of measured agents attempting to manage the flow of information to measurers. Under this interpretation, GAO results must be considered artificially inflated. According to the model presented in this book, organizations the GAO studied would have censored areas where their responses would have been less favorable in an effort to guard the status gained as a winner or finalist of the Baldrige.

The GAO insists that the low response rate does not introduce bias into their results because findings were reinforced by on-site interviews at the twenty companies. Whether the audits produce biased results is also hotly contested by advocates of SCEs. Terry Bollinger and Clement McGowan (1991) claim that SCE measures *are* subject to subversion by those being measured. They argue that "the current grading system is so seriously and fundamentally flawed that it should be abandoned rather than modified" (p. 40), and that the incentive to achieve a high rating is very strong. Like the GAO, defenders of SCEs (for example, see Humphrey and Curtis, 1991) cite their on-site interviews as a means of eliminating bias introduced by those being measured. But, as was noted in Chapter Eight, there is ample reason to think that correction for bias attempted by informal contact with the organization is unlikely to be effective. In his interview, Tilford recounted the tale of his organization's encounter with SCE auditors, saying, "if we wanted to, we could blow them away. . . .they would walk out of there thinking we were far greater than we really were."

Whatever one may believe about the tendency of measurement systems to become dysfunctional, in the context of the model and explanation of dysfunction presented in this book, some burden of proof seems to shift toward the proponents of potentially dysfunctional methods. As Deming, Tilford, DeMarco, and some others have observed, measurement systems introduce costs that must be taken into account. Proponents of these systems are far too casual in assuming that costs are outweighed by benefits. They should be obliged to make their case explicitly. The net benefit of measurement systems is not self-evident. As in many situations, the debate could move to a new level by earnest consideration of the assumptions that underlie some particular points of view.

The Nature of the Measurement Problem

One feature of the model deserves highlighting, not only because it may seem to be a shortcoming of the model (it is not), but also because it is interesting. In the model, the customer is the final arbiter of the value of the agent's effort allocation. In some cases this assumption may seem to pose some conceptual difficulties.

A firm that buys a component part from another firm is surely a customer in some sense. Yet it has been assumed that the buying firm cannot judge the value of the component—that honor is reserved for the buying firm's customer. It is reasonable to ask what is special about the principal's customer that allows him to judge value, given that the principal cannot judge value when she acts as a customer to an agent in, for example, procuring a product component.

This question is easily answered, however, by considering the customer in the model to be an "end consumer." A customer can finally judge value if he or she is the end consumer of the product or service in question. Another question that then arises is why the end consumer can assign blame to a firm for engaging in opportunistic behavior during production of a product or provision of a service, given that the firm cannot do the same for its agents. Again, the question is not profound. As the product nears completion (that is, nears readiness for consumption), responsibility for its value is assumed by the last principal among the principals and agents who participated in production. When the product is finally marketed, a consumer who has problems with the product will be able to point to a particular manufacturer as the entity from whom he bought the product. The end consumer, then, is in a unique position to judge value and to hold opportunistic firms accountable.

The producer, however, often has no similar advantage with respect to his suppliers.[3] In tracking down the problem, he must confront a network of agents, each of whom did some work and many of whom are candidate problem-causers. The tests of product value available to the principal are, for reasons outlined earlier, usually mere proxies for true tests of acceptance by end consumers. As products grow more complex and involve more agents, the principal's problem grows more serious and vulnerability to agent opportunism also grows. The existence of this difference between end and interim customers is apparent upon noting that customers do not often seek to impose production monitoring on the firms from whom they intend to buy.[4] The cus-

---

[3] This is not to say the producer never faces an unambiguous situation where value can easily be judged and blame for problems can be easily attributed. These are, of course, measurement-friendly situations.

[4] There are exceptions, of course. Whenever the end customer is also coordinating the production process, he or she begins to experience the problems of the principal in evaluating value. For example, someone coordinating the building of his own house would not be a pure end customer in the sense of the model, because he suffers from the same attributional difficulties that a principal does.

tomer knows he has final authority to judge value and that the manufacturer is responsible for correcting problems; the principal's difficulties in pinning down the source of problems is not the customer's concern.

Technological advances and their associated increases in product and service complexity are causing opportunities for covert opportunism to migrate toward the end of the production cycle, thus complicating the judgment of value even by the end customer. Suppose that the product in question is a word-processing software package that will eventually be mass-marketed. Because it is large, many agents—employees, independent contractors, and the like—must be involved in its production. Early in the cycle of production, the value of the product can be tested in only a limited way. As larger and larger pieces are completed, value can be tested in increasingly meaningful ways, as pieces are fitted together and tested for intermediate functions. However, because of the complexity of the product, when a problem is discovered, its source is far from obvious.

Two problems prevent attribution of the problem to a particular agent. First, it is difficult, bordering on impossible for intellectual work, to determine who did what. This moves attribution of blame away from fact finding and toward the political realm, toward lobbying for interpretations of what happened. The second problem is that product components interact in complex ways, so it may not be apparent which part of the product is causing the problem. Even if attribution were possible, the problem cannot be pinned down well enough to blame anyone.

Suppose a customer's word processor runs under a window-based operating system and his printer has internal software of its own. Suppose further that the customer has a problem printing documents—perhaps he cannot get his word processor to print in italics. At least four problems might be occurring. There might be a problem with the printer software, or with the operating system's print manager, or with the word processor itself. Or, the problem might be the result of an interaction of choices made independently by two of the producers. Suppose also that printer, operating system, and word-processing software were each developed by a different company. On contacting each, the customer may find that, for example, the word-processing company blames the operating system, the operating-system company blames the printer software, and the printer company blames the word-processing software. The average customer has no way to evaluate the conflicting claims. Thus, even at this very late point in the production cycle, there are vulnerabilities to covert opportunism. Problems like this would be expected to proliferate as the computer filled up with software. The problem is inherent in the nature of the production task, in its intense intellectual, knowledge-specific character. Other products that share this character also share these problems.

Chapter Eighteen:

Societal Implications and Extensions

Many implications of this study have been discussed already. There are three more, however, that are too important not to mention explicitly and that deserve more attention than the space remaining allows. All have the potential to shift the ground under prevailing beliefs about social phenomena.

The first has to do with how the model in this book forces reconsideration of the feasibility of enforcing human behavior in a broad realm of social, not just organizational, situations. Specifically, there is an extent to which long-standing notions of sanction-based social contracts (see Hobbes, 1651, for example) are undermined when individual behavior is as hard to observe and enforce as the model suggests. Threat of verification backed by sanctions ceases to explain much of the contractual performance that is commonly observed in the world. It becomes difficult to defend claims that promised retribution forces civility and that potential punishment deters criminal acts.

The U.S. criminal justice system provides ample evidence of dysfunction in sanction-based social systems (see, for example, Skolnick, 1966). Common interpretations of dysfunction in criminal justice suggest that the incompetence of bureaucrats, the dishonesty of lawyers, and the leniency of judges keep the system from working correctly. In the context of this study, such interpretations sound much like the assertions by software measurement experts and practitioners that organizational measurement would work well if only it could be correctly implemented. An alternative suggestion is that the dysfunction arises because the system is designed based on faulty assumptions about the observability of behavior.

Several questions arise from this suggestion. How do our laws work, then? Or do they? Why are they obeyed as exactly as they are? Or are they? One interpretation of the model is that situations in which people *can* engage in undetectable opportunism are widespread. So, surely laws cannot work in the way conventionally believed, for example, causing people to behave civilly because they fear the consequences of not doing so. To the extent that a system of laws provides imprecise incentives (think of the tax code), it even encourages dysfunctional (that is, uncivil) behavior. From a purely external motivation standpoint, given that the incentives created by laws are almost certainly imperfect, civility in social settings (if one believes it is really there) seems to arise not because of laws but in spite of them. Viewed more broadly, however, taking internal motivation into account, laws must surely play a role in codifying the criteria that establishes identification with a social group. Laws, then, may function less as interlocking threats and more as prescriptions of social ritual. They express not so much the terms of a social contract as they describe the steps in a social dance in which people tend to want to participate. What happens, then, to a society and its laws when people stop wanting to dance the same dance or belong to the same groups? The obvious answer—that the society becomes uncivil, even violent, and the laws, which never worked as deterrents anyway, ineffective—is chilling because it seems confirmed by the daily newspapers.

Probabilistic Measurement

Before writing off the deterrent effects of laws, however, one should consider another extension of this work. It has been assumed in constructing the model that there exist tasks that will not be observed because they are too costly to observe. But it is worth considering what might happen if the high price of observing hard-to-observe dimensions were occasionally paid. Observation on a dimension would be infrequent because measurement on the dimension is so costly, but even the small probability that measurement will occur creates an expectation in the minds of agents that might cause them to allocate effort to that high-cost dimension. External incentive effect might be realized even on dimensions where cost of measurement is very high.

To the extent that some laws have a deterrent effect, it is probably achieved in this manner. In many cases, people conform to laws even when they know they cannot be enforced, because of internal motivation, devotion to moral codes, and the like. When they are affected by promises of punishments, however, it is probably because they think that there is some probability of an investigation that will reveal information on a dimension not usually monitored. This is true in the case of societal laws when the people believe that law enforcement is not particularly cost sensitive, that some investigations will be carried out even when they cannot be justified on a cost-benefit basis. There is casual empirical evidence that legal proceedings do continue past the point where they net financial benefit. Robert Frank (1988) has suggested that cooperation in society is often enforced by threats of responses based on principle or other less than strictly economic motivations. When people behave opportunistically with respect to the law, though, they often do so in a way that is consistent with the predictions of the model. Real-estate developers may ignore ordinances from which variances cannot easily be detected, for example.

This notion of *probabilistic* measurement might also be seen as a way of rescuing motivational measurement from the disrepute bestowed on it by the model. If agents were inclined to behave as if full supervision were realized out of fear of a low probability check on high measurement cost dimensions, then systems of measurement would work much more as they do in airplane cockpit analogies, and the like. The simplistic notions of measurement-based control might seem vindicated. The problem with this position, though, is that most systems of measurement explicitly do not threaten investigation on difficult-to-measure dimensions. In some cases, there are explicit or implicit guarantees that the agent will be measured only in accordance with the agreed-upon criteria. Such guarantees may be legally enforced (such as in wrongful dismissal proceedings). The whole idea behind a measurement-based merit pay system, for example, is that the agent is told exactly what constitutes performance. Such systems seek to drive out the sort of ambiguity that might serve as a deterrent against opportunistic behavior in the minds of agents.

Nevertheless, an interesting extension of this work would be to consider the special circumstances in which there is an implicit threat that measurement might occur on any dimension, at any time. Such an extension would be important in an attempt to use the model in this book to study the deterrent effects of laws. As has been discussed, the model here suggests that the ability of institutions to enforce behavior is much more limited than is commonly believed. But if citizens do fear probabilistic measurement of high cost dimensions, then laws might regain some of their intended incentive effect. Other societal structures are worth studying in the context of the contention that incentives do not operate well in some circumstances.

Another implication that deserves further study concerns the role of consultants (that is, non-organizational agents) in organizational efforts. The cynical explanation of dysfunction suggests that consultants, who are not members of the group and are therefore less motivated internally to achieve group objectives, benefit from installation of measurement systems that are conceptually attractive but actually dysfunctional. Conceptual attractiveness makes a consultant's suggestions sellable—it gets him in the door. Dysfunction permits consultants to control measures of their own performance, thus preserving their credibility and their flow of income. This is a much stronger statement than the common observation that organizations and their consultants have incentives that are not exactly aligned. The cynical explanation suggests that wares peddled by consultants are more likely to be both conceptually attractive and dysfunctional than similar wares that arise from other sources (for example, from workers within the firm). Paul Krugman (1994) argues similarly in criticizing the effects that consultants—he calls them "policy entrepreneurs"—have had on U.S. economic policies in recent decades.

Firm Integration Theories

A final set of implications of the model and explanations presented here concerns economic theories that attempt to explain firm integration. It remains at least mildly embarrassing for the science of economics that its main theories provide so little justification for the existence of one of the most common features of the economic landscape—the large, multi-division firm. R.H. Coase (1937) first crystallized the central question in this area by observing that organizations are simply an alternative to the market mode of production and by asking what determines the mode of production that arises in any given case. Coase invokes the notion of transaction costs—the costs of using the price mechanism that derive from bargaining, especially on long-term contracts—to explain why firms come into being. He argues that a firm, unlike a market, can forego use of the price mechanism by assigning an individual (a supervisor) the authority to instruct other parties to the transaction (employees). The amount of bargaining is thereby reduced, lowering transaction costs. On the other hand, markets enjoy cost advantages over firms because of a lesser propensity toward administrative rigidity. Costs of organizing are set against the costs of using the price mechanism in an ongoing analysis; a firm organizes where the former costs are lower.

Coase gets more credit for raising the question of why firms exist than for providing the answer, however. Some have observed that there appears to be a conceptual weakness in the Coase argument (Hart, 1989). It is instructive to consider the conceptual weakness because a broader version of it is arguably shared by all of the theories thus far developed in this area. The broader version of the weakness can be expressed as a question: Why does simply organizing into a firm provide advantages that could not be realized by constructing similar arrangements between firms? Arguments that seek to explain firm integration inevitably point to features of organization that supposedly lower costs in some way. But it is virtually always possible to argue that these features could be replicated in an inter-firm arrangement.

For example, Armen Alchian and Harold Demsetz (1972) proclaim the firm's ability "to settle disputes by fiat, by authority, or by disciplinary action superior to that available in the conventional market [is] a delusion" (p. 777). Within markets or firms, there are only two forms of punishment for a person who does not comply with an agreement: "withholding future business or seeking redress in the courts" (Alchian and Demsetz, loc. cit.). These are exactly the same within or across firms. Firing an employee (or, if you are an employee, quitting) and refusing to do business with another market firm are exactly equivalent, as are the abilities in each case to take legal action.[1] Alchian and Demsetz suggest instead that the firm achieves lower transaction costs because it is easier to observe and attribute agent efforts within a firm than it is across firms. Improved ability to observe agent activities comes from the closer physical proximity and familiarity that tends to accompany the organizational mode of production.

It is not difficult to see, however, that Alchian and Demsetz's theory suffers from the same broad weakness as the Coase theory. Physical proximity and familiarity can be brought about via a long-term contract that specifies collocation of the two involved firms. Much more could be said about the strengths and weaknesses of the Alchian and Demsetz theory. What is important to note here is the pattern in the institutional economics literature. A theory of firm integration is proposed that points to certain features of the organization as the source of cost advantages. Subsequently, another theorist observes that the feature in question is not unique to organizational production and that, in fact, there are market production arrangements that also have the same feature. Such a theorist usually then puts forth another theory that shares the same broad weakness.

Williamson (1975, p. 29) offers a set of advantages that firms have over markets. He argues that 1) organizing permits economizing due to the evolution of efficient procedures and languages of exchange; 2) internal business units are less able and less apt to behave in a way that maximizes one unit's interests at the expense of other internal business units; 3) firms have audit capabilities superior to those of markets because company auditors have more extensive access to production information; and 4), as Coase suggests, the firm's capacity to settle disputes by fiat is an advantage over markets. Sanford Grossman and Oliver Hart (1986) offer a theory based on property rights. The important insight in

---

[1] Williamson (1975) has observed that courts refuse to hear certain within-firm disputes that they would consider if they were inter-firm disputes. So, there is perhaps some difference in one's ability in firms and markets to take legal action. But this fairly narrow set of activities seems an unlikely explanation for the existence of the firm.

their work is that ownership of an asset, under the laws of our society, entitles one to control the asset to the extent that control has not been explicitly yielded in the terms of a contract. When a situation occurs that was unanticipated, argue Grossman and Hart, the owner of an asset has the right to dictate how the asset will be used. The cost advantage in organizing, then, arises from ownership of these *residual rights* to determine use of an asset.

There is inadequate space here to fairly address all the above theories, each of which is impressive in its own way. All of the proposed theories of firm integration seem to have a ring of truth about them. What is worrisome, however, is that the earlier discussed weakness peers out from beneath most, if not all, of them. Take Williamson's theory, for example: Why could not efficient codes of exchange arise between firms involved in a long-term contract? Surely they sometimes do. Why could not superior audit procedures be written into a long-term contract? Surely they sometimes are. Or, take the Grossman and Hart theory of property rights: How does authority over the residual uses of property allow an owner more influence over humans involved in production? The laws of our society do not permit control of human assets (that is, slavery); bargaining between parties (employees and supervisors) is therefore hardly eliminated. It is not obvious how property rights even reduce bargaining, especially in knowledge-intensive industries in which the primary assets are human ones. How much power does a law firm have over its lawyers simply because it owns the desks at which they sit? Surely not very much.

One of Williamson's points has not yet been addressed. Williamson argues that within firms agents are less able and less apt to take advantage of colleagues. The reason for lesser ability is not clear because explanations of it suffer from the discussed broad weakness. But the assertion that agents within firms are less apt to seek selfish advantage is more interesting. Here is where the model and explanations in this book can come into play by offering a suggestion: The advantage that organizations have over markets may be due to their increased ability to delegate and their ability to eliminate distortion by convincing agents to forego opportunities for self-interested guile.

This advantage of organizing is different in nature from the advantages proposed by economic theories because it flows from sociological and psychological characteristics of the situation, not tangible structural features. One obvious truth cannot be avoided: There is one certain difference between being within a firm and being outside it that can never be replicated by a long-term contract—the difference of belonging to the organizational group. Members of an organization see themselves as part of a group, which, according to the model proposed here as well as the experiments of Dawes (1991) and the suggestions of Simon (1991) and Ouchi (1981) among others, makes a difference in their tendencies to engage in covert opportunism. This is an area that needs much more investigating. The remarkable findings of Dawes *et al.* (1988) about the power of group identity to induce cooperation and the unlikely factors that lead to group identity are a potential cornerstone for a new theory of firm integration.

The Difficulty of Explaining Cooperation Under Assumptions of Pure Self-Interest

This book adds to a clamor of voices suggesting that assumptions of pure self-interest are inadequate to explain observed levels of cooperation. It has been argued here that a great many production processes are vulnerable to covert opportunism by involved agents. It follows that when agents are productive in situations where rational agents would not be, there is something other than pure self-interest at work. This book has suggested that whatever is at work (and it is probably related to group identity), it is very likely worth studying and trying to cultivate in real organizations.

Economists, who have traditionally favored models based on pure self-interest, are also coming around to the view. Arrow (1971) notes that there is general advantage in moral behavior (behavior not motivated by narrow self-interest) in many exchanges between firms and between employers and employees, and that such behavior occurs. In the work of Williamson (1975, 1985), it is possible to discern a progression in which narrow self-interest is gradually found to be more and more wanting as an explanation of behavior within firms. In this spirit, the comments of Alchian and coauthor Susan Woodward (1988), in a review of Williamson's *The Economic Institutions of Capitalism*, are appropriate to close this chapter:

> We believe it is important to recognize the forces of ethics, etiquette, and "proper, correct, reasonable, moral, etc." standards of conduct in controlling business relationships. We do not believe contracts are observed (e.g., self-enforcing) only so long as the personal economic costs of contract violations exceed expropriable rents obtainable by violations. People do not always violate contracts whenever their own costs are less than their own gains from violation. Temptations of free-riding or stealing are resisted even when the net gains of free-riding or stealing are great. We don't know enough about how such "moral" forces operate to say more than that they exist and should not be ignored in seeking an understanding of how the economic institutions of capitalism, or any other -ism, evolve and operate (p. 77).

Chapter Nineteen:

A Difficult But
Solvable Problem

I once presented some of the ideas in this book to a group that had just been assembled to develop a software measurement system for a large organization. The group's members had been carefully selected. They were some of the organization's brightest and most energetic people, and many had software measurement experience.

These people listened attentively and often nodded knowingly as I spoke of dysfunction and its causes. But, as I enumerated the difficulties of the measurement problem, I sensed that my audience was becoming uneasy. Faces seemed to be darkening. Finally, while I was analyzing a particularly spectacular example of dysfunction, one person could contain his growing discomfort no longer: "But you're being so negative!" he protested.

Although I don't believe that the contents of this book are essentially negative, the book's message can seem quite stern. A reader hoping to find, say, a three-step program for measurement success, encounters instead a detailed description of the difficulties involved in establishing a successful measurement program. Perhaps frustration is an inevitable first reaction to facing squarely the true difficulty of the measurement problem.

The fundamental message of this book is that *organizational measurement is hard*. The organizational landscape is littered with the twisted wrecks of measurement systems designed by people who thought measurement was simple. If you catch yourself thinking things like, "Establishing a successful measurement program is easy if you just choose your measures carefully," watch out! History has shown otherwise. I urge you to regard all such statements as skeptically as you might regard the statement "that pistol is not loaded."

The first step to solving the measurement problem is facing its true difficulties. If you feel frustration, push past it and formulate a plan for dealing with the difficulties. Successful plans may have what seem like extreme elements. For example, it might be necessary to enforce very strict requirements on the acceptable use of measurement. Managers might need to satisfy themselves with less access to data than they want, to preserve the validity of the data they are permitted to see. Most of all, organizational leaders will have to work twice as hard as they might like to establish a culture conducive to measurement, in which measurement is seen as a useful way to learn but not as the be-all and end-all of performance management.

A good test of whether you are succeeding in creating the right kind of culture is to ask yourself what seems to be driving the people around you to do a good job. Is the motivation of workers primarily internal or external? That is, are people in your organization driven primarily by feelings of identification with the organization and their fellow team members? Do they work hard because they don't want to let their coworkers down? Or, are they driven mostly by a desire to do well on their next performance review and get a big raise? Strive for the former, but be prepared that, too often, measurement systems produce the latter.

The difference between these two types of motivation is important because of what is perhaps the most basic problem of organized activity. In a typical organization, an individual worker confronts tens or hundreds of small decisions every day. In making each decision, he can choose to do what is best for the organization or he can choose what is best for himself. As I have written repeatedly, what is best for the organization almost never is exactly the same as what is best for the worker's measurement performance. So, if the worker feels that the measurement system is of greatest importance, then each of his decisions will be at least a little worse than it might have been if he had felt compelled to choose what is best for the organization. Add this effect across many workers and the result is significant. Often, it is the difference between transitory and lasting success for the organization. An organization can try to keep its measurement systems and other formal criteria aligned with its overall goals, but this is a difficult and expensive process at best.

The good news is that you *can* succeed in producing a culture conducive to measurement. There are organizations in which people seem to have given themselves completely to the pursuit of organizational goals, at least temporarily, organizations in which members hunger for measurement as a tool that helps get the job done. In these settings, there is nothing special about measurement; measurement seems neither remarkable nor threatening. To use measurement inappropriately would betray a sacred trust, and no one would consider such a betrayal.

I know it is possible to create such a culture. I have worked in organizations and on teams that have achieved this higher state. Maybe you have worked in similar settings. If so, you know that this kind of culture is precious for reasons that go far beyond the benefits that can be realized from a successful measurement program. You may also know that this kind of culture is fragile and often fleeting. So, when you achieve it, I urge you to guard it fiercely, because if you lose it, it is distressingly difficult to regain.

Appendix:

Interview Methods and Questions

I nterviews with eight experts were arranged in three ways. First, five have affiliations of varying immediacy with the Software Engineering Institute of Carnegie Mellon University in Pittsburgh, Pennsylvania, and were contacted through that organization. The nature of SEI affiliations ranged from close to quite distant (for example, serving twice a year on SEI Steering Committees). Of the three experts who were not contacted through the SEI, two were suggested by other experts' recommendations and the third was contacted through completely independent means. These experts participated voluntarily, receiving no money or any other form of payment. Four other experts were approached but declined to participate, all citing time constraints.

Experts were first contacted by telephone or electronic mail. Four interviews were carried out in person and four by telephone. Interviews took between thirty-five minutes and one hour. I conducted all interviews, which were audio recorded and transcribed. An interview template was followed strictly in that all questions were asked of all experts, but unscripted follow-ups to provide clarifications were frequent. Interviews were open-ended, but every attempt was made to assure that the interviewee addressed the intent of each question. This often involved repetition of questions and some elaboration of the intent of questions, usually at the request of the expert. Also, they were told that they could respond to any question by declaring that they had addressed the question in an earlier response; experts rarely exercised this option. When scripted questions were finished, I probed issues of relevance to the model more directly with unscripted follow-up questions, to verify that the experts had intended what they said in responses to earlier questions. Experts reviewed the interview transcripts to correct transcription errors, but in no case did a change alter the meaning of a response. Interview transcripts were also sanitized to remove names or specific references that might reveal the identity of organizations associated with experts, as requested by the experts.

The interview template was constructed to move from the general to the specific, to prompt comment on issues central to the model while avoiding revelation of the content of the model. The model provides specific answers to some interview questions; expert responses can be compared to model responses on these questions. A coding scheme was used to indicate the distance between the responses of the model and each expert's responses. On each question, 2 was scored for perfect or nearly perfect agreement with the model, 1 with incomplete but in-spirit agreement, and 0 for either no agreement or disagreement with the model. The questions that are the focus of the coding scheme and how the model answers those questions are given in the following:

1. *What do you see as the purpose(s) of software metrics?*

   To agree with the model, experts should cite informational uses, and, perhaps, cautiously qualified motivational uses. If motivational uses are cited, so should dangers be; also, there should be some statement of the importance of not overextending targets.

2. *What are the advantages to an organization of using metrics?*

   For agreement with the model, informational uses and cautiously qualified motivational uses should be cited. Dangers of overextended targets in partial supervision should be cited.

3. *What are the disadvantages to an organization of using metrics?*

Many answers are possible, but full agreement with the model requires mention here of the danger of dysfunction.

4. *Should software metrics report status on individual projects? For example, should software metrics alert managers when a project is behind schedule?*

Experts could agree with the model by saying "no," because project measurements reflect on project managers and identifiable groups capable of colluding to subvert measurements. Agreement could also be indicated by saying "yes" if the response were accompanied by emphatic insistence on ways to protect project managers and groups from evaluation by project measures.

5. *Should software metrics be used to control the development process?*

If experts cited process refinement or coordination uses here, they were in agreement with the model. If they took control to have motivational implications and approved, they were not in agreement.

6. *Should software metrics be used to motivate employees?*

The model specifies a strong "no" answer to this question; very cautious positive responses that illustrate great concern for the delicacy of using motivational measurement might indicate partial agreement.

7.   *We have talked about three (perhaps more) uses for metrics: status reporting, process control, and motivation. Can metrics do all three of these (and any other uses you might think of) at the same time? Explain.*

The model specifies a "no" answer unless the expert has defined motivation to mean something other than what it means in the context of this book.

8.   *Is it possible to use metrics in only one sense (for example, process control) without also using them in other ways (for example, motivation, status reporting, and so on)? Is there a reason to do this, or should all uses of metrics be pursued simultaneously?*

Agreement with the model requires that this question elicit a discussion of the incompatibility of motivational and informational uses of measurement, and the desirability of decoupling informational and motivational measurement.

The next section in the interview template was designed to elicit 1) whether "comprehensiveness" of measures is an issue, and 2) if it is, whether the expert believes that it is possible to construct a comprehensive measurement system for software development. These two questions were not actually asked because informal pretests of the interview template revealed that people tend to answer "yes" regardless of their underlying beliefs. "Comprehensive" just sounds like a good thing for measurement systems to be. To solve this problem, the answers to the questions were elicited more subtly, by asking questions that pretests showed to elicit responses more in line with true beliefs. The answers to the two questions of central concern (rather than those actually asked) are provided here, however.

9. *Is comprehensiveness of measures an issue of relevance to the effectiveness of measurement programs?*

   Model dictates a "yes" answer to this question.

10. *Is it possible for measures to be comprehensive in software development?*

    Model dictates a "no" or "not in most cases" response.

11. *What sorts of reactions from their employees should be expected by organizations that implement metrics?*

    Model: Concern about motivational uses and attempts to subvert measures.

12. *Based on your beliefs and/or experience, do developers welcome metrics? If so, why and under what conditions?*

    Model: Metrics may be welcomed when procedural safeguards are in place to prevent motivational use of information.

13. *Based on your beliefs and/or experience, do developers resist metrics? If so, why and under what conditions?*

    Model: Metrics are resisted and subverted when there are no strict procedural safeguards.

14. *It has sometimes been noted that measuring people can produce unintended consequences. How serious is this problem when the measurements are software metrics?*

    Model: Very serious.

15. *How concerned are you that developers might divert efforts from what is not measured to what is measured?*

Model: Very concerned.

Experts were asked in the next section of the template to state the degree to which they agree with the following statements:

16. *Metrics make developers do what they are supposed to do.*

Model: Disagree.

17. *Developers resist change, and metrics give them an incentive to try things in new ways.*

Model: Disagree.

18. *Developers don't know what the customer wants; metrics are a way of showing them.*

Model: Disagree.

19. *Developers do the best they can, but they need feedback to understand how well they are doing their jobs.*

Model: Agree.

20. *Metrics provide managers with a way of identifying employees who are especially strong or weak performers.*

Model: Disagree.

21. *Metrics provide managers and developers with a way of defending themselves when things go wrong.*

Model: Agree.

In addition to the questions directly asked, the answers to five questions were obtained by evaluating the aggregate response of each expert. These questions address major differences between what the model recommends and what a person who has succumbed to the dysfunctional mistake portrayed in the earnest explanation of dysfunction might recommend. The questions are denoted X1–X5; X-Scores were tabulated separately and also included in the overall Total Score for each expert. X-Scores reflect the degree to which the expert emphasized points similar to those of greatest importance in the model.

X1. *Did the expert ever mention the problem of accidental attribution of blame or credit to individuals or identifiable groups, especially project managers or groups, with whom it is hard not to associate measurements?*

Model agreement requires that this issue be mentioned.

X2. *Did the expert ever make a statement that suggested approval of schemes that link measurement with reward or punishment in any software development circumstances?*

Model agreement requires that the expert make no or very qualified favorable mention of motivational uses of measurement for software development.

X3. *Did the expert ever mention the tendency of measurement programs to evolve into something undesirable and other than what was originally intended?*

Model agreement requires that this is a major concern.

X4. *Who, according to the expert, is the main audience for measurement information?*

Model agreement requires that workers, and not higher-level managers, are the main recipients of measurement information.

X5. *Does the expert emphasize the need for procedural—that is, more than mere promises—protection against motivational uses of measurement?*

Model agreement requires that the expert insist on procedural measures to prevent motivational uses of measurement.

Glossary

Agency Theory

A branch of economic theory devoted to the construction of rigorous mathematical representations of organizational arrangements between principals (employers or owners) and agents (employees).

Agent

An individual role within an agency model that supplies the labor (effort) required for a productive enterprise. An agent works for a principal. Think of an agent as an employee.

Critical Dimension (of Effort)

An aspect of a job to which effort must be devoted if the resulting work is to have any value at all. If no effort is devoted to a critical dimension, then no value to the customer can result.

Customer

The final arbiter of the value of all effort allocations by the agent. The one and only judge of the value of a final product.

Delegatory Management

A style of management that relies on the internal motivation and the personal standards of quality of employees. Rather than precisely specifying duties and measuring progress against what is specified, delegatory managers let their employees define their own ways of working and their own ways of achieving organizational goals. Input and inspiration come from the manager. Contrast delegatory management with measurement-based management.

Disutility

A term used by economists to mean, roughly, displeasure or dissatisfaction derived from an activity. The opposite of utility.

Dysfunction

Results of an organizational activity that are opposite or interfere with intended results. Results that are dysfunctional often fulfill the letter of stated intentions but dramatically depart from the spirit of an organizational directive or objective.

Effort

A resource supplied by agents as they work. Effort is not quite the same thing as time, because an agent can spend time without working hard. It is something like the multiplication of time spent by intensity of work.

Full Supervision

A way of managing an agent in which every critical dimension of effort is measured and performance targets are set on all critical dimensions.

Informational Measurement

Measurement valued entirely for what it tells about an organizational process. Organizational measurement is used to learn from and to plan. It is not intended to produce behavioral changes in organization members.

Measurement-Based Management

A style of management that relies on specification of objectively verifiable work standards and measurement of compliance with the standards. Contrast measurement-based management with delegatory management.

Motivational Measurement

Measurement valued entirely for its ability to motivate and change behavior. Motivational measurement is used to quantify the value of compensation for compliance with objectively verifiable standards of work.

No Supervision

A way of managing an agent in which no dimension of effort is measured. The agent is left to work on his own, according to his own standards of achievement.

Partial Supervision

A way of managing an agent in which some but not all critical dimensions of effort are measured. Partial supervision is the most common situation in real organizations. It is also more subject to dysfunction than any other way of supervising.

Principal

An individual role within an agency model, responsible for supplying the investment and facilities for a productive enterprise. A principal hires and directs the work of an agent. Think of a principal as a manager or an employer.

Unsupervised Effort Allocation

The allocation of effort that will be chosen by an agent in the absence of any external incentives, purely as a result of internal motivation.

Utility

A term used by economists to mean, roughly, pleasure or satisfaction derived from an activity. The opposite of disutility.

Bibliography

"A-12 Too Far." *The Economist* (January 12, 1991), p. 24.

Ackoff, Russell L. "Towards a System of Systems Concepts." *Management Science*, Vol. 17, No. 11 (1971), pp. 661–71.

Alchian, Armen A., and Harold Demsetz. "Production, Information Costs, and Economic Organization." *The American Economic Review*, Vol. 62, No. 5 (December 1972), pp. 777–95.

Alchian, Armen A., and Susan Woodward. "The Firm Is Dead; Long Live the Firm, A Review of Oliver E. Williamson's *The Economic Institutions of Capitalism*." *Journal of Economic Literature*, Vol. 26 (March 1988), pp. 65–79.

Anderson, Erin. "The Salesperson as Outside Agent or Employee: A Transaction Cost Analysis." *Marketing Science*, Vol. 4, No. 3 (Summer 1985), pp. 234–54.

———, and David Schmittlein. "Integration of the Sales Force: An Empirical Examination." *Rand Journal of Economics*, Vol. 15, No. 3 (Autumn 1984), pp. 385–95.

Argyris, Chris. *The Impact of Budgets on People.* New York: Controllership Foundation, 1952.

———. *Integrating the Individual and the Organization*. New York: John Wiley & Sons, 1964.

———. *Management and Organizational Development: The Path from XA to YB*. New York: McGraw-Hill, 1971.

Aristotle. *Poetics*. (Original, circa 335 B.C.) Excerpts from *Aristotle's Theory of Poetry and Fine Art*, trans. S. Butcher, 3rd ed. London: Macmillan, 1902. Reprinted in *Dramatic Theory and Criticism: Greeks to Grotowski*, ed. Bernard F. Dukore, pp. 31–56. New York: Holt, Rinehart and Winston, 1974.

Arrow, Kenneth J. *Essays in the Theory of Risk-Bearing*. Chicago: Markham Publishing, 1971.

———. "The Economics of Agency," in *Principals and Agents: The Structure of Business*, eds. John W. Pratt and Richard J. Zeckhauser, pp. 37–51. Boston: Harvard Business School Press, 1985.

Barnard, Chester I. *The Functions of the Executive*. Cambridge: Harvard University Press, 1938.

Basili, V.R., and D.M. Weiss. "A Methodology for Collecting Valid Software Engineering Data. " *IEEE Transactions on Software Engineering*, Vol. SE-10, No. 6 (November 1984), pp. 728–38.

Beach, Jr., Chester Paul. "A-12 Administrative Inquiry." Memorandum for the Secretary of the Navy. Washington, D.C.: Department of the Navy, 1990.

Berliner, Joseph S. "A Problem in Soviet Business Management." *Administrative Science Quarterly*, Vol. 1 (1956), pp. 86–101.

Blau, Peter M. *The Dynamics of Bureaucracy: A Study of Interpersonal Relations in Two Government Agencies*, 2nd ed. Chicago: The University of Chicago Press, 1963.

———, and W. Richard Scott. *Formal Organizations: A Comparative Approach*. San Francisco: Chandler Publishing, 1962.

Boehm, B.W. *Software Engineering Economics.* Englewood Cliffs, N.J.: Prentice-Hall, 1981.

Bollinger, Terry B., and Clement McGowan. "A Critical Look at Software Capability Evaluations." *IEEE Software*, Vol. 8 (July 1991), pp. 25–41.

Boyett, Joseph H., and Henry P. Conn. "Developing White-Collar Performance Measures." *National Productivity Review* (Summer 1988), pp. 209–18.

Brennan, Ed. "An Open Letter to Sears Customers." *USA Today* (June 25, 1992), p. A8.

Brody, D. *Workers in Industrial America.* Oxford, Eng.: Oxford University Press, 1980.

Brooks, Jr., Frederick P. "No Silver Bullet: Essence and Accidents of Software Engineering." *IEEE Computer*, Vol. 20, No. 4 (April 1987), pp. 10–19. Reprinted in DeMarco and Lister, eds., 1990, pp. 14–29.

Campbell, Donald. "Assessing the Impact of Planned Social Change." *Evaluation and Program Planning*, Vol. 2 (1979), pp. 67–90.

Campbell, N.R. *Foundations of Science.* New York: Dover Publications, 1957. Excerpt reprinted in Mason and Swanson, pp. 254–55, as quoted by Flamholtz, 1979.

Chambers, R.J. "Measurement and Misrepresentation." *Management Science*, Vol. 6, No. 2 (1960), pp. 141–42. Reprinted in Mason and Swanson, pp. 161–68.

Chandler, Alfred. *The Visible Hand: The Managerial Revolution in American Business.* Cambridge: Belknap Press of Harvard University Press, 1977.

Chew, W. Bruce. "No-Nonsense Guide to Measuring Productivity." *Harvard Business Review* (January-February 1988), pp. 110–18.

Coase, R.H. "The Nature of the Firm." *Economica* (November 1937), pp. 386–405.

Coombs, C., and G. Avrunin. "Single-Peaked Functions and the Theory of Preference." *Psychological Review,* Vol. 84 (1977), pp. 216–30.

"The Cracks in Quality." *The Economist* (April 18, 1992), pp. 67–68.

Crosby, Philip B. *Quality Is Free.* New York: McGraw-Hill, 1979.

————. Letter. *Harvard Business Review* (January-February 1992), pp. 127–28.

Cummings, L.L., and Randall B. Dunham, eds. *Introduction to Organizational Behavior: Text and Readings.* Homewood, Ill.: Richard D. Irwin, 1980.

Curtis, Bill, Herb Krasner, and Neil Iscoe. "A Field Study of the Software Design Process for Large Systems." *Communications of the ACM,* Vol. 31, No. 11 (November 1988), pp. 1268–87.

Curtis, Bill, Herb Krasner, Vincent Shen, and Neil Iscoe. "On Building Software Process Models Under the Lamppost." *Proceedings of the Ninth International Conference on Software Engineering,* pp. 96–103. Washington, D.C.: IEEE Computer Society Press, 1987.

Dawes, R.M. *Rational Choice in an Uncertain World.* Fort Worth, Tex.: Harcourt Brace Jovanovich, 1988.

————. "Social Dilemmas, Economic Self-Interest, and Evolutionary Theory." In *Recent Research in Psychology: Frontiers of Mathematical Psychology: Essays in Honor of Clyde Coombs,* eds. Donald R. Brown and J.E. Keith Smith, pp. 53–92. New York: Springer-Verlag, 1991.

————, and J.M. Orbell. "A Simpson's Paradox Analysis of Why Cooperation Can Be a Personally Advantageous Behavior in Optional, Non-Repeated Negotiations Without Words." (Paper presented at the Stanford Center on Conflict and Negotiation on Barriers to Conflict Resolution, February 13-14, 1992.)

——, and A.J.C. van de Kragt. "Not Me or Thee but We: The Importance of Group Identity in Dilemma Situations: Experimental Manipulations." *Acta Psychologica*, Vol. 68 (1988), pp. 83–97.

"The Death of Corporate Loyalty." *The Economist* (April 3, 1993), p. 63.

DeCharms, R. *Personal Causation: The Internal Affective Determinants of Behavior.* New York: Academic Press, 1968.

Deci, E.L. "Effects of Externally Mediated Rewards on Intrinsic Motivation." *Journal of Personality and Social Psychology,* Vol. 18 (1971), pp. 105–15.

——, and R.M. Ryan. *Intrinsic Motivation and Self-Determination in Human Behavior.* New York: Plenum Press, 1985.

Degroot, Morris. *Optimal Statistical Decisions.* New York: McGraw-Hill, 1989.

DeMarco, Tom, and Timothy Lister. *Peopleware: Productive Projects and Teams.* New York: Dorset House Publishing, 1987.

——, eds. *Software State-of-the-Art: Selected Papers.* New York: Dorset House Publishing, 1990.

Deming, W. Edwards. *Out of the Crisis.* Cambridge, Mass.: MIT Press, 1986.

Devin, L. Private communication, Swarthmore College, 1983.

"Diary of an Anarchist." *The Economist* (June 26, 1993), p. 66.

Drucker, Peter F. *The Practice of Management.* New York: John Day, 1954.

Eccles, Robert G. "The Performance Management Manifesto." *Harvard Business Review* (January-February 1991), pp. 131–37.

——, and Philip J. Pyburn. "Creating a Comprehensive System to Measure Performance." *Management Accounting* (October 1992), pp. 41–44.

Festinger, L.A. *A Theory of Cognitive Dissonance.* Evanston, Ill.: Row, Peterson, 1957.

Fisher, Lawrence M. "Sears's Auto Centers to Halt Commissions." *The New York Times* (June 23, 1992), p. C1.

Flamholtz, Eric G. "Toward a Psycho-Technical Systems Paradigm of Organizational Measurement." *Decision Sciences,* Vol. 10, No. 1 (January 1979), pp. 71–84. Reprinted in Mason and Swanson, pp. 253–66.

Fouhy, K., G. Samdani, and S. More. "ISO 9000: A New Road to Quality." *Chemical Engineering* (October 1992), pp. 43–47.

Frank, Robert. *Passions Within Reason: The Strategic Role of the Emotions.* New York: W.W. Norton, 1988.

Frey, Bruno S. "Motivation as a Limit to Pricing." *Journal of Economic Psychology,* Vol. 14 (1993), pp. 635–64.

Friedman, Milton. *Essays in Positive Economics.* Chicago: University of Chicago Press, 1953.

Gabor, Andrea. "Catch a Falling Star System." *U.S. News and World Report* (June 5, 1989), pp. 43–44.

Gardiner, J. *Traffic and the Police: Variations in Law-Enforcement Policy.* Cambridge: Harvard University Press, 1969.

Garvin, David A. "How the Baldrige Award Really Works." *Harvard Business Review* (November-December 1991), pp. 80–93.

———. "Building a Learning Organization." *Harvard Business Review* (July-August 1993), pp. 78–91.

Gasko, H. "You Can Earn ISO 9002 Approval in Less Than a Year." *Journal for Quality and Participation* (March 1992), pp. 14–19.

Grady, Robert B., and Deborah L. Caswell. *Software Metrics: Establishing a Company-wide Program.* Englewood Cliffs, N.J.: Prentice-Hall, 1987.

Grossman, Sanford, and Oliver D. Hart. "The Cost and Benefits of Ownership: A Theory of Vertical and Lateral Integration." *Journal of Political Economy*, Vol. 94, No. 4 (1986), pp. 691–719.

Grove, H., T. Mock, and K. Ehrenreich. "A Review of HRA Measurement Systems from a Measurement Theory Perspective." *Accounting, Organizations, and Society*, Vol. 2, No. 3 (1977), pp. 219–36. Quoted in Flamholtz.

Hannaway, Jane. "Higher-Order Thinking, Job Design and Incentives: An Analysis and Proposal." (Working paper, 1991.)

Hart, Oliver. "An Economist's Perspective on the Theory of the Firm." *Columbia Law Review*, Vol. 89, No. 7 (1989), pp. 1757–74. Reprinted in Williamson, 1990, pp. 154–71.

Hauser, John R., and Don Clausing. "The House of Quality." *Harvard Business Review* (May-June 1988), pp. 63–73.

Healey, James R. "California: Sears 'Loots' Auto Center Customers." *USA Today* (June 12, 1992), p. B1.

Hillkirk, John. "Tearing Down Walls Builds GE: CEO Welch Shapes a Culture of Openness, Teamwork." *USA Today* (July 26, 1993), p. B2.

Hirsch, F. *The Social Limits to Growth.* Cambridge: Harvard University Press, 1976.

Hobbes, Thomas. *Leviathan.* New York: Dutton, 1950. (Original, 1651.)

Holmström, Bengt. "On Incentives and Control in Organizations." Ph.D. Thesis, Stanford University, 1977.

———. "Moral Hazard and Observability." *The Bell Journal of Economics*, Vol. 10 (Spring 1979), pp. 74–91.

———, and Paul Milgrom. "Multitask Principal-Agent Analyses: Incentive Contracts, Asset Ownership, and Job Design." *Journal of Law, Economics, and Organizations*, Vol. 7 (Spring 1991), pp. 24–52.

Hopwood, A. *Accounting and Human Behavior*. Englewood Cliffs, N.J.: Prentice-Hall, 1974. Quoted in Flamholtz, reprinted in Mason and Swanson, p. 261.

Humphrey, Watts S. *Managing the Software Process*. Reading, Mass.: Addison-Wesley, 1989.

————, and Bill Curtis. "Comment on 'A Critical Look.'" *IEEE Software* (July 1991), pp. 42–46.

Humphrey, W.S., and W. Sweet. *A Method for Assessing the Software Engineering Capability of Contractors*, CMU/SEI-87-TR-23, ESD-TR-87-186. Pittsburgh: Software Engineering Institute, 1987.

Ishikawa, Kaoru. *What Is Total Quality Control? The Japanese Way*, trans. David J. Lu. Englewood Cliffs, N.J.: Prentice-Hall, 1985.

Jensen, Michael C., and William H. Meckling. "Theory of the Firm: Mangerial Behavior, Agency Costs and Ownership Structure." *Journal of Financial Economics*, Vol. 3 (1976), pp. 305–60.

Kadane, Joseph B., and Patrick D. Larkey. "Subjective Probability and the Theory of Games." *Management Science*, Vol. 28, No. 2 (February 1982), pp. 113–20.

Kaplan, Abraham. *The Conduct of Inquiry*. San Francisco: Chandler, 1964. Quoted in Mason and Swanson, p. 517.

Kaplan, Robert S., and David P. Norton. "The Balanced Scorecard—Measures That Drive Performance." *Harvard Business Review* (January-February 1992), pp. 71–79.

Kelvin, Lord. Quoted in Humphrey, 1989.

Kerr, Steven. "On the Folly of Rewarding A, While Hoping for B." *Academy of Management Journal*, Vol. 18, No. 4 (1975), pp. 769–83. Reprinted in Cummings and Dunham, pp. 459–70.

Kohn, Alfie. "Why Work Incentives Fall Down on the Job." *USA Today* (December 16, 1993), p. A13.

Krugman, Paul. *Peddling Prosperity: Economic Sense and Nonsense in the Age of Diminished Expectations.* New York: W.W. Norton, 1994.

Larkey, Patrick D., and Jonathan Caulkins. "All Above Average and Other Unintended Consequences of Performance Appraisal Systems." (Paper presented at the National Public Management Research Conference, Technology and Information Policy Program, The Maxwell School, Syracuse University, September 1992.)

Latham, Gary P., and Edwin A. Locke. "Goal-Setting—A Motivational Technique That Works." In Cummings and Dunham, pp. 153–64.

Leavitt, Barbara, and James G. March. "Chester I. Barnard and the Intelligence of Learning." *Annual Review of Sociology,* Vol. 14 (1988), pp. 319–40. Reprinted in Williamson, 1990, pp. 11–37.

Leavitt, Tom. "The Pluralization of Consumption." *Harvard Business Review* (May-June 1988), pp. 7–8.

Lee, C. "The New Employment Contract." *Training* (December 1987), pp. 45–56.

Lehman, M.M. "Process Models, Process Programs, Programming Support," *Proceedings of the Ninth International Conference on Software Engineering,* pp. 14–16. Washington, D.C.: IEEE Computer Society Press, 1987.

Lepper, M.R., and D. Greene, eds. *The Hidden Costs of Reward: New Perspectives on Human Behavior.* New York: Erlbaum, 1978.

Levinthal, Daniel. "A Survey of Agency Models of Organizations." *Journal of Economic Behavior and Organizations,* Vol. 9, No. 2 (March 1988), pp. 153–85.

Lewis, Robert W. *A Case Study of Management Planning and Control at General Electric.* New York: Controllership Foundation, 1955. Excerpt reprinted in Mason and Swanson, pp. 213–23.

Liker, Jeffery K., Rajan R. Kamath, Nazli Wasti, and Mitsuo Nagamachi. "Supplier Development in Product Development in Japan and the U.S." Ann Arbor, Mich.: University of Michigan, 1993. (Working paper.)

Likert, Rensis. *New Patterns of Management.* New York: McGraw-Hill, 1961.

———. *The Human Organization: Its Management and Value.* New York: McGraw-Hill, 1967.

McFadyen, T., and T. Walsh. "Is ISO 9000 Worth the Paper It's Written On?" *Journal for Quality and Participation* (March 1992), pp. 20–23.

McGraw, K.O. "The Detrimental Effects of Reward on Performance: A Literature Review and a Prediction Model." In Lepper and Greene, pp. 33–60.

McGregor, Douglas. *The Human Side of Enterprise.* New York: McGraw-Hill, 1960.

March, James G. "Notes on Ambiguity and Executive Compensation." *Scandinavian Journal of Management Studies* (August 1984), pp. 53–64.

———, and Herbert A. Simon. *Organizations.* New York: John Wiley and Sons, 1958.

Marquardt, D. "ISO 9000: A Universal Standard of Quality." *Management Review* (January 1992), pp. 50–52.

Mason, Richard O., and E. Burton Swanson, eds. *Measurement for Management Decision.* Reading, Mass.: Addison-Wesley, 1981.

Merton, Robert K. "The Unanticipated Consequences of Purposive Social Action." *American Sociological Review,* Vol. 1 (1936), pp. 894–904.

———. *Social Theory and Social Structure,* enlarged ed. New York: The Free Press, 1968. (Original edition, 1957.)

"Musical Chairs." *The Economist* (July 17, 1993), p. 67.

Osterweil, Leon. "Software Processes Are Software Too," *Proceedings of the Ninth International Conference on Software Engineering,* pp. 2–13. Washington, D.C.: IEEE Computer Society Press, 1987.

Ouchi, William G. "A Conceptual Framework for the Design of Organizational Control Mechanisms." *Management Science,* Vol. 25, No. 9 (September 1979), pp. 833–48.

———. *Theory Z: How American Business Can Meet the Japanese Challenge.* Reading, Mass.: Addison-Wesley, 1981.

———. *The M-Form Society: How American Teamwork Can Recapture the Competitive Edge.* Reading, Mass.: Addison-Wesley, 1984.

Peat Marwick Main. *1988 Report on Executive Compensation.* 1988.

Pfeffer, J. "Converging on Autonomy: Anthropology and Institutional Economics." In Williamson, 1990, pp. 72–97.

Porter, Michael E. "Capital Disadvantage: America's Failing Capital Investment System." *Harvard Business Review* (September-October 1992), pp. 65–82.

Pratt, John W., and Richard J. Zeckhauser, eds. *Principals and Agents: The Structure of Business.* Boston: Harvard Business School Press, 1985.

Ridgway, V.F. "Dysfunctional Consequences of Performance Measurements." *Administrative Science Quarterly,* Vol. 1, No. 2 (September 1956), pp. 240–47.

Roesthlisberger, F., and W. Dickson. *Management and the Worker.* Cambridge: Harvard University Press, 1939.

Rohlen, Thomas P. *For Harmony and Strength: Japanese White-Collar Organization in Anthropological Perspective.* Berkeley, Calif.: University of California Press, 1974.

Ross, Steven A. "The Economic Theory of Agency: The Principal's Problem." *The American Economic Review,* Vol. 63, No. 2 (1973), pp. 134–39.

Schaffer, Robert H., and Harvey A. Thomson. "Successful Change Programs Begin with Results." *Harvard Business Review* (January-February 1992), pp. 80–89.

Semler, Ricardo. *Maverick!* New York: Warner Books, 1993.

Shafritz, Jay M., and J. Steven Ott, eds. *Classics of Organization Theory,* 2nd ed., Pacific Grove, Calif.: Brooks/Cole Publishing, 1987.

Simon, Herbert A. "On the Concept of Organizational Goal." *Administrative Science Quarterly,* Vol. 9 (1964), pp. 1–23.

———. *Reason in Human Affairs.* Stanford, Calif.: Stanford University Press, 1983.

———. "Organizations and Markets." *Journal of Economic Perspectives,* Vol. 5, No. 2 (Spring 1991), pp. 25–44.

Singer, Max. "The Vitality of Mythical Numbers." *The Public Interest,* Vol. 23 (Spring 1971), pp. 3–9. Reprinted in Mason and Swanson, pp. 416–21.

Skolnick, J. *Justice Without Trial: Law Enforcement in Democratic Society.* New York: John Wiley and Sons, 1966.

Software Engineering Institute. "Process Program Releases Revised Capability Maturity Model: An Interview with Bill Curtis." *Bridge* (December 1991), pp. 18–22.

Software Productivity Consortium Services Corporation. *Software Measurement Guidebook.* SPC-91060-CMC. Herndon, Va.: SPC, 1992.

Stake, Robert E. "Testing Hazards in Performance Contracting." *Phi Delta Kappan* (June 1971), pp. 583–89.

Staw, Barry M. "Counterforces to Change," *Change in Organizations,* ed. Paul Goodman. San Francisco: Jossey-Bass, 1982.

Stevens, S.S. "On the Theory of Scales of Measurement." *Science,* Vol. 103 (1946), pp. 677–80. Quoted in Flamholtz, reprinted in Mason and Swanson, pp. 71–84.

Sugarman, Carole. "U.S. Produce Standards Focus More on Appearance Than Quality." *The Pittsburgh Press* (August 5, 1990), p. E1.

Taylor, Frederick Winslow. "The Principles of Scientific Management." In Shafritz and Ott, pp. 66–81. (Originally published in *Bulletin of the Taylor Society,* December 1916.)

Thompson, James D. *Organizations in Action.* New York: McGraw-Hill, 1967.

Tuchman, Barbara. *The March of Folly from Troy to Vietnam.* New York: Alfred A. Knopf, 1984.

Tully, Shawn. "Your Paycheck Gets Exciting." *Fortune* (November 1, 1993), pp. 83–98.

U.S. General Accounting Office. "Management Practices—U.S. Companies Improve Performance Through Quality Efforts." Washington, D.C.: GAO, May 1990.

Vroom, Victor H., and Edward L. Deci, eds. *Management and Motivation.* Middlesex, Eng.: Penguin Books, 1970.

Weinberg, Gerald M., and Edward L. Schulman. "Goals and Performance in Computer Programming." *Human Factors,* Vol. 16, No. 1 (1974), pp. 70–77.

White, Leonard D. *The Republican Era, 1869-1901: A Study in Administrative History.* New York: Macmillan, 1958.

Whitt, Ward. "Uniform Conditional Stochastic Order." *Journal of Applied Probability,* Vol. 17 (1980), pp. 112–23.

Williamson, Oliver E. *Markets and Hierarchies: Analysis and Antitrust Implications.* New York: The Free Press, 1975.

————. *The Economic Institutions of Capitalism: Firms, Markets, Relational Contracting.* New York: The Free Press, 1985.

————, ed. *Organization Theory: From Chester Barnard to the Present and Beyond.* New York: Oxford University Press, 1990.

"Your Company Wants You . . . For Now." *The Economist* (July 17, 1993), pp. 13–14.

Author Index

Subject Index